Social Media in Libraries

SOCIAL MEDIA IN LIBRARIES

Editor
Sandhya Aggarwal

Ess Ess Publications
New Delhi

Social Media in Libraries

ISBN: 978-81-7000-797-5

First Published 2016

Published by:
Ess Ess Publications
4831/24, Ansari Road,
Darya Ganj,
New Delhi-110 002.
INDIA
Phones: 23260807, 41563444
Fax: 41563334
E-mail: info@essessreference.com
www.essessreference.com

Cover Design by *Patch Creative Unit*

Printed and bound in India at Salasar Imaging Systems.

CONTENTS

Foreword

Preface

1. Role of Social Media in Future Libraries 1
   H.S. Chopra
2. Application of Social Media through Open Source Software "KOHA" 14
   Sandhya Aggarwal
3. Usage of E-Resources from Academic Libraries to Social Media 25
   Jagjit Singh
4. Use of Social Networking in Libraries as Tool for Information Sharing and Services 32
   Rajeev Manhas
   Asha
   Sapna Rani
5. How Social Media is Currently Used by Librarians 41
   R S Aswal
6. Social Media and Library Service 46
   Bibhash Kumar Mishra
7. Social Media Marketing 53
   Gurpreet Kaur
8. Usage of Blogs in Libraries 61
   Jagjit Singh

9. Benefits of Institutional Repositories in the Society 73
Amandeep Kaur

10. Library 2.0 81

11. Impact of Social Media in Marketing of Library Product and Services 88
Shaveta

12. Digital Library Services With Social Networking 94
Ashu Tyagi

13. Library Classification in the 21st Century 109
Jivesh Bansal

FOREWORD

The world is an ever changing and most dynamic place. The ingredients of most of the changes and dynamism are Information, Knowledge and Technology. With the advent of modern technologies of handling information and knowledge, there has been a drastic change in the approach of individuals and institutions towards libraries and information centres. To cope-up with this changing scenario, the libraries and information centres are now required to improve and adapt themselves with all of these technological changes, so that they may be able to provide an ampoule of desired information in the most satisfactory way.

Often, I get opportunities to write something for a group of professionals and indeed it gives me immense pleasure to share some of my thought contents related to wonderful world of information and library science. I am very pleased to mention here that this book has not only covered many facets, but also the treatment and indulgence with which they have been revelled with. I am also happy to see many of the authors from the information handling community who I am proud to say have excelled in their chosen areas.

The delivery of information through Internet and allied technologies has made the 'global village' concept a reality. The emergence of social networking and its adaption by the majority of the people has revolutionized the field of document sharing and delivery because of its low cost and instant delivery and accessibility. All our libraries must try to use these types of tools to enhance the usability

The adaption of these tools will also help libraries professionals to communicate, participate and add value by accessing and sharing knowledge from available sources.

Prof. Sandhya Aggarwal, a young, enthusiastic library professional has done an excellent job in the field of library & information science by setting -up library & information science department in the college. This edited work of hers is another contribution which will provide guidelines for librarians and information sciences professionals to move from traditional to modern libraries.

I congratulate her for her excellent editorial work and wish her a great success in life.

Rajeev Manhas
Chief Librarian
Baba Farid University of Health Sciences,
Faridkot – 151 203 (Punjab) India

Preface

Technology is advancing day by day, consequently environment is also changing.

As it has been rightly said that "*Change is the law of nature*".

Libraries should find strategies of sustaining relevance without changing the role of the library. The advent of new technologies has changed the scene in the information world. Today, information is available at the users' fingertips through social media. Social media can be a Trojan horse for library. New technologies shorten the distance between the library users and the rest of the world through tools and sites such as YouTube, Facebook, Twitter, and Pinterest. It is a real-time connection, where user can subscribe to other users' activities, and share new ideas and technology. This book attempts to introduce new technology, how library can stand up in future social world with its aims and rules, and with its strategic planning, how it (new technology) can be used effectively, how a user can access this world of information. As today, mostly everyone including librarian already exists in social media world. Generally, people watch or comment on a YouTube video, like a friends' facebook, update and read your colleagues blog, then they are using social media, but they don't necessarily know how to use social technologies effectively and meaningfully. In our research endeavours also, we can utilize social media to share our work with our colleagues and work collaboratively in more efficient ways.

I want to express my gratitude to colleagues, experts, professionals, and scientists, who always encouraged me and contributed their highly informative and insightful articles for this elegant book.

My thanks are no less due to Ess Ess Publications, New Delhi, who made the publication of the book possible in such a short time. I shall feel amply rewarded if this book renders help to those, who are concerned with library as an Institution.

— Editor

1

Role of Social Media in Future Libraries

H.S. Chopra
Ph. D.(History), Ph.D.(Library & Information Science)
University Librarian, Guru Nanak Dev
University Library, Amritsar (Pb), India.

In every age human being was having some knowledge and he wanted to communicate his ideas to others. Undoubtedly the present social media has come from a long lineage of primitive predecessors. In ancient India messages were sent through emissaries, soldiers, messengers, servants and village security personnel. They used chariots, horses, camels and pigeons for delivering urgent and important messages at the earliest. During Maurya period because of stability and development a proper communication system was established[1]. One comes across messages written on leaves and stones, preserved as visual relics of an era when images and symbolic representations were the order of the day. Flute music was signifying the ideas of gestures. The sound of drumbeats and crude bushfires were additionally used to transmit messages across rivers and valleys. In old Hindu scriptures there are references to 'carriers of messages'. In Oriental civilization of Egypt 4000 years ago, there was a proper postal system for delivering messages[2]. Cloth, paper, bhurjapattar, palm leaves etc. were used for transmitting information from one person to other.During the Medieval and Mughal period 'Halkaras' were the message carriers[3].

Most successful communication system was that of Persians during 540 B.C. Darius extended the network of roads throughout his empire in order to control the empire. Herodotus marvels at this fast communication system. Roads were so well prepared that messenger could travel about 200 miles a day[4].

Cicero (52 B.C.) used to write letters on papyrus rolls which were exchanged, commented and copied. In those days there was no paper and no printing presses even then information was circulated. His speecheswere copied and distributed. Several letters were read loudly. Basically it was the beginning of social media. Transmission was through human powered network[5].

With the advent of Internet the messages through e-mail have totally minimized the role of postal system and made an end of 163 years old Telegram. Mobile industry has rapidly covered the urban, rural, the rich and the lower income people. Instant messages, photos, videos through WhatsApp havechanged the social life of the People.

Social media are computer-mediated tools that allow people to create, share and exchange information, ideas and pictures/videos in virtual communities and networks.

Social media, the most popular media in the present age, is attracting the users irrespective of age and surprisingly the user's time spent on it has almost doubled. Social media unlike the past, has reached millions of people within no time, but with accuracy, longevity and affordability.

Keeping in view the types of social media we can consider magazines, weblogs, wikis, social blogs, microblogging, social networks, podcasts, photographs, pictures, videos etc. Music sharing, voice messages are now common medias. Social media can be defined of space-timers, space locators, quick times and slow times. Marketing, sales promotion are taking maximum benefit from social media.

1. Space-timers (location and time sensitive): Exchange of messages with relevance for one specific location at one specific point in time (e.g., Facebook Places; Foursquare)

2. Space-locators (only location sensitive) : Exchange of messages, with relevance for one specific location, which are tagged to a certain place and read later by others (e.g.,Yelp; Qype)

3. Quick-timers (only time sensitive) : Transfer of traditional social media applications to mobile devices to increase immediacy (e.g., posting Twitter messages or Facebook status updates)

4. Slow-timers (neither location, nor time sensitive) : Transfer of traditional social media applications to mobile devices (e.g., watching a YouTube video or reading a Wikipedia entry)[6]

E-banking, e-commerce are alsomaking maximum use of social media.Difference from other media can be in quality, reach, frequency, accessibility, usability, immediacy and permanence[7].

Difference between community media i.e. Radio, Television, print newspaper etc. and social media is apparent. Social media can be considered as an open arena where anybody can participate and the complete universe is approachable.

SOCIAL SITES

Ten years ago there was no Facebook, Instagram, YouTube or Twitter. Mark Zukerberg, a student of Harvard University, changed the entire scenario of social life. No one can deny that social media from fad has gone to phenomena.

Facebook's earliest form Facemash was started by Mark Zuckerberg, a Harvard University student alongwith his three classfellows Andrew McCollum, Chris Hughes and Dustin Moskovitz. Facebook as such became very popular within few years. In August 2008 total active users were 100 million; in 2010 the user's number reached 500 million. In 2013 the users were more than 1230 million[8].

Twitter is an online social networking service that enables users to send and read short 140 character messages called 'Tweets'. Registered users can read and post tweets, but unregistered users can only read them. Users access Twitter through the website interface, SMS, or mobile device app. It was created by Jack Dorsey, Evan William, Biz Store and Noah Glass and by July 2006 it was launched. By December 2014 Twitter has more than 500 million users. Twitter has its own bird logo[9].

Microblogging is a broadcast medium that exists in the form of blogging. A microblog differs from a traditional blog in that its content is typically smaller in both actual and aggregated file size. Microblogs allow users to exchange small elements of content such as short sentences,. Individual images or video links. The related concepts are Live logging and Instant blogging. Live blogging is derivative of Microblogging that generates a continuous fed on a specific web page. Instant messaging are such as available, offline, away, busy etc.

LINKED IN

It is a business oriented site. In 2013 LinkedIn reports more than 259 million acquired users in more than 200 countries and territories. The founders were Reid Hoffman, Allen Blue, K. Guericke, Eric Ly and Jean – Luc Valli out. India is the second major country after United States with highest number of users. USA has 93 million whereas India has 24 million.

Social media has reached new heights within three to four years. Messages on net solve a number of problems. Google, Facebook, Amazon, Apple, LinkedIn are running a race to prove more useful to the users[10].

USERS OF SOCIAL MEDIA

Number of users of Social Media all over the world is increasing at a rapid speed. About 17.3% of people are using social media in the world.

Active Monthly Users of the 'Big 9'

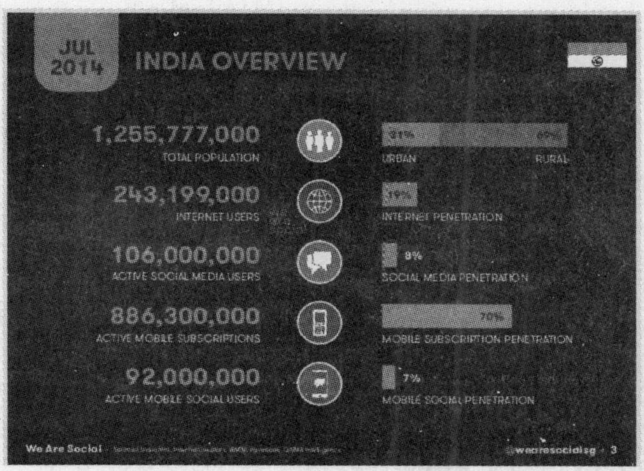

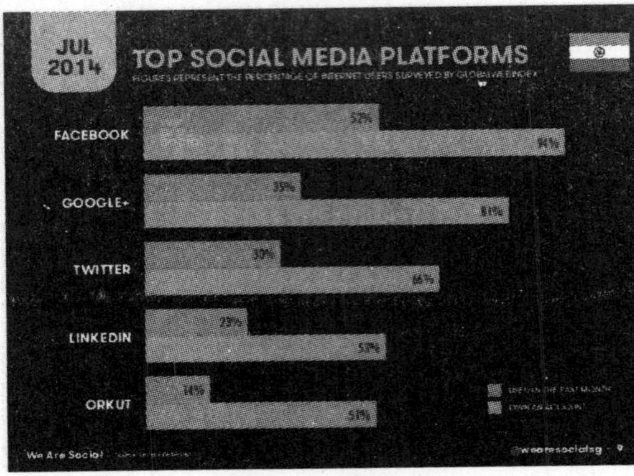

IMPACT OF SOCIAL NETWORKING/MEDIA

SNS social networking sites are providing jobs and avenues for marketing. In India certain online shopping sites have given employment to a large number of unemployed. undoubtedly certain people are misusing it too. India is multilingual country but English is widely used. In U.K. majority of the youngster age 16 to 24 years old 75% of them post messages on Internet.

Number of users of social media are increasing at a rapid pace. Nearly 80% adults are online and out of them about 60% are using social sites. More Americans get their news on Internet. Comparatively newspapers in print[11].

SOCIAL MEDIA MINING

Social Media Mining is the process of representing, analyzing, and extracting actionable patterns from social media data. Social Media Mining, introduces basic concepts and principal algorithms suitable for investigating massive social media data; it discusses theories and methodologies from different disciplines such as computer science, data mining, machine learning, social network analysis, network science, sociology, ethnography, statistics, optimization, and mathematics. It encompasses the tools to formally represent, measure, model, and mine meaningful patterns from large-scale social media data[12].

Social media shatters the boundaries of the real world and the virtual world. We can now integrate social theories with computational methods to study how individuals interacts and how communities form. The uniqueness of social media data calls for novel data mining technique that can effectively handle users generated content with rich social relations. The study and development of these now techniques are under purview of social media mining, an emerging discipline under the umbrella of data mining. Social media mining is the process of representing, analyzing, and extracting actionable patterns from social media data.

Social media mining cultivates a new kind of 'Data Scientist' who is well versed in social and computational theories. New techniques will be evolved for solving social theories and data. Social media data is undoubtedly very big.

There are many categories of social media including, but not limited to, social networking (Facebook or LinkedIn), Microblogging (Twitter), Photo-sharing (Flicker, Photobucked or Picasa), News aggregation (Google reader, Stumble upon or Feed burner), Video sharing (You Tube, Metacafe), Livecasting (Ustream or Justin, TV), Virtual worlds (Kaneva), Social gaming (World of Warcraft), Social search (Google, Bing or Ask.com) and instant messaging (Google Talk, Skype, Yahoo! Messenger).

The first social media site was Geocities in 1994. SixDegree.com was the first social networking site.

These individuals form a virtual world in which individuals (social atoms), entities (content, sites etc) and interactions (between individuals and entities) coexist. Social norms and human behaviour govern this virtual world. By understanding these social norms and models of human behaviour and combining them with the observations and measurements of this virtual world, one can systematically analyze and mine social media. Social media in a computable way measures it and designs models that can help us understand its interactions[13].

POSITIVE EFFECTS OF SOCIAL MEDIA

In the book "Networked – The new social operating system" by Lee Rainie and Barry Wellman, the two authors reflect on mainly positive effects of social media and other internet based social networks. According to the authors, social media are used to document memories, learn about and explore things, advertise oneself and form friendships. For instance, they claim that the communication through internet based services can be done more privately than in real life. Everybody has the possibility to become a content creator. Content creation provides networked individuals opportunities to reach wider audiences. Moreover, it can positively affect their social standing and gain political support. This can lead to influence on issues that are important for someone. As a concrete example of the positive effects of social media, the authors use the Egyptian revolution in 2011, where people used Facebook to gather meetings, protest actions, etc[14].

Content creation is a voluntary and participatory act. What is important is that networked individuals create, edit and manage content in collaboration with other networked individuals. This way they contribute in expanding knowledge. Wikis are examples of collaborative content creation.

CRITICISM OF SOCIAL MEDIA

Trustworthiness and reliability are two factors which need attention. The users cannot believe that it is absolute correct or fabricated. Twitter is increasingly a target of heavy activity of marketers. Their actions, focused on gaining massive numbers of followers, includes use of advanced scripts and manipulation techniques that distort the prime data of social media by abusing human trustfulness. Andrew Keen has criticized social media in his book 'The Cult of the Amateur'. He has criticized Web 2.0 for being similar to Marxism, for destroying professionalism and for making it impossible to find high quality material amidst all of the user-generated web content. Google is like a parasite which does not create any contents at its own but give links to other sites. Any visit to Wikipedia means lessening of actual research. It is creating Pseudo scholars who depend on sometimes wrong, incomplete, incorrect English and spellings. 'What is free is actually costing us a fortune'. Social media is threating copy right issues, ideas of authorship and intellectual property rights. The information which we receive is regulated and analyzed by some gatekeepers of search engines. 'Moral values and cultural honesty is at stake because of social media. Social sites are becoming infested with anonymous sexual predators and pedophiles thus our human values and family culture is deteriorating[15].

According to Erik Qualman, Social media has affected the inefficient marketing, reduced the print marketing and finished the middleman. Million dollar television marketing has dwindled to very low stage. Now the people are referring to products and services on social media. Marketing by 'word of mouth' was very slow and had to face language problems, boundaries of the countries etc. 'Word of mouth' goes 'World of Mouth' because of latest information communication technology. Global connectivity, reviews of products, messages of relatives etc. are in digital form. We no longer search for the news. It finds us, people want easy access to their news[16].

Wikipedia's success and downfall of Encyclopedia

Britannica is a matter of technology and the easiness to access the contents.

FUTURE OF SOCIAL MEDIA

Once upon a time, there was no Facebook, Twitter, Instagram or YouTube. Our lives did not revolve around a stream of status updates, tweets, videos and filtered photos. That was just 10 years ago.

We saw the dramatic impact social media wielded four years ago. It was a tool that helped spark the Arab Spring—a democratic civil uprising in the Middle East that began in Tunisia in December 2010 that helped force rulers from power in such countries as Tunisia, Egypt and Libya. Thanks to Twitter and other social media, people were able to protest and raise awareness in the face of repression. The revolution continues.

Fast-forward to the future, and we should see global social media usage continue on its upward trajectory. In just four years, eMarketer projects it will nearly double by 32.7 percent. By then 2.44 billion of the world's population will be on social networks.

"When news breaks in the future, it will be covered by a multitude of eyewitnesses streaming live video. These streams will knit together into a single immersive video, enabling the viewer to virtually experience the event in real time. For better or worse, the world will feel like it's right around the corner."

Mobile is the first step toward the portable future of social media. What we're seeing now in the industry is at the tip of the iceberg in terms of sharing our personal experiences. We're already seeing increased personalization, more individual-to-individual communication.

"Twenty-five years from now, the way in which we both input and observe media will have completely shifted. Keyboards on desktops, laptops, tablets and smartphones will become increasingly irrelevant, as interactions on what was once called social media will largely be voice-controlled. Holographic displays will be shifting into the mainstream, making the debate between the benefits of a 4-inch vs. a 4.7-inch smartphone display a thing of the past."

"My bet is that social will be less about standalone apps and websites and more about the "piping" of the Internet. In the future the Internet will operate more like electricity does today, as an unseen part of the infrastructure around us that we notice only when it's not present. This will put more pressure on advertisers, marketers, and big thinkers to spread their messages in a genuinely interesting and useful way, since they'll be less able to rely on interruptive display ads to get people's attention.

"The term social media will fade out and become a mass media form in 25 years." Social media in the future. It will become part of the fabric of our clothes, part of the glasses we wear and the shoes we put on, and the gadgets we no longer see as gadgets but as part of our very selves. Social will measure, but sharing will become more passive in the process; it won't require any effort on our part to share any part of our lives[17].

LIBRARIES AND SOCIAL MEDIA

Time and technology never stop. From clay tablets to paper was a long journey but creation of paper created a great revolution. Printing Press ended the era of scribes. Now the internet is going to finish the printed books and Journals. Social media has also ushered new medias for the students. Videos of various lectures are available for the viewers. However their authenticity is to be ensured. Most of prominent professors and the scholars are uploading their lectures. School, college and university lectures are available. Music, songs, films, advertising etc. are also available on videos.

Question arises the libraries will use social media for its services. Technology should be taken for the help of libraries and librarians. The computer and internet have proved very useful to the libraries. Now the social media is to be used for the services of the libraries. The Librarian should think beyond the four walls of the library. The different social platforms give freedom to Librarians to write what they like. Libraries in digital era should use Facebook, Twitter, Flicker, YouTube etc. for the promotion of library activities, library rare photographs, seminars, proceedings of the meeting, seminar, conference or workshop, lecture or training.

Information driven society can never move without social media nor the librarians.

REFERENCES

- RomilaThapar, A History of India Vol. I, New Delhi, Penguin Book, p.384.
- Will Durant, Our Oriental Heritage, New York, Simon & Schuster, 1935.
- William Kvine, The Decline and Fall of the Mughal Empire
  - *see also*
  - *http://Shodhganga.Inflibnet.ac.in/8080/jspui*
- *http://en.wikipedia/org/wiki/Darius_I*
  - *see also*
  - ShapurShahbazi, Darius I the Great, Encyclopedia Iranica Vol. 7, New York, Columbia University, 1996, p.47.
- Maria Popova, Cicero's Web: How Social Media Was Born in Ancient India
  - *see also*
- See Wikipedia, Social Media
- Ibid.
- *http://en.wikipedia.org/wiki/History_of_Facebook*
- Twitter *http://en.wikipedia.org/wiki/Twitter*
- *http://ourstrong.linkedIn.com*
- *http://en.m.wikipedia.org/wiki/Social_Media*

- Reza Zefarani, Mohammad Ali AbbasiHuan Liu and Social Media Mining, Cambridge University Press, 2014, pp. 21-41.
- Ibid., pp. 21-31.
- *http://en.m.wikipedia.org/wiki/Social_Media*
- Andrew Keen, The Cult of the Amateur: How Today's Internet is Killing on Culture, Currency, 2007.
- Eric Qualman, Socionomics, Wiley, 2012.
- Mary Cutherine, Predictions on the Future of Social Media.
  * *http://en.m.wikipedia.org/wiki/Social_Media*

2

Application of Social Media through Open Source Software "KOHA"

Sandhya Aggarwal
Librarian & HOD in BLISc
M.M.P.G.College,Fatehabad

ABSTRACT

Today everyone is rapidly using Facebook, YouTube etc. in daily life from the last decade. But these are being used on individual level on Internet, not through any organization or institution. Most of the users and librarians are not aware of such facilities. Thus this article explores and highlights how a librarian can give the facility of various media available over the Internet, eg Delicious, Facebook etc. and how the libraries can introduce the users with new services and enriching existing services.

INTRODUCTION

When we think, to share and improve the users' interest and to attach with new technologies of web, we should have knowledge of social media and software. Birdsall (2007) is of opinion that web 2.0 is a social movement. Web services are often referred to as "social media" due to their role in supporting communication and building online communities. Social media is the use of web based and mobile technologies to turn communication into interactive dialogue. Davis (2005) expresses web 2.0 not as a technology but as an attitude. But we say that it's not only as a technology but also as an attitude because users are choosy to use the blog, chatting etc. Nowadays, the concept of social media is not new but it has become common for all to create profiles, to advertise products and services. By using this technology, reputation and standard of libraries can be improved and enhanced. These tools and techniques can broadly be grouped into five categories:

i) **Synchronous communication :** Instant Messaging

ii) **Content Delivery :** RSS Feed, HTML Feed, Streaming Media, Podcasting, Vodacasting, and SMS enquiry services

iii) **Collaborative Publishing Tools :** Blogs and Wikis

iv) **Collaborative Service Platforms :** Social Networks, Tagging, Social Bookmarking Services

v) **Hybrid Applications :** Mashups, AJAX, and API

What are the necessary steps to start social media with KOHA

As a product under continuous improvement during the era of web 2.0 KOHA has introduced a number of features that enhance the user's library experience. Web based online public access catalogue system allows the public to search the catalogue in the library and at homes. Web centric architecture, no additional software or utility is required for web, access through the browser Mozilla Firefox only. Customization is provided. Here we will discuss about the application of social media through opensource software "KOHA".

1) Go to System Preferences in "Administration"
2) Open the "OPAC" preference
3) Enable the OPACBaseURL
4) After it, enable the "SocialNetworks"

After setting these preferences, there will appear new options of social media, which allow the users to link the bibliographic records with theirFaceBook, Twitter, Delicious etc. and allow to email the record.If social media is strategically planned and implemented, libraries can reap many benefits of using social media.

WEB SERVICES WITH KOHA

1. Cataloguing
2. Marketing of Services
3. User Education
4. Current Awareness Service
5. Selective Disseminative of Information
6. Reference Service
7. Display Board
8. Podcast
9. Picture
10. Share with bibliographic record
11. Self-check-in and renewal of book
12. Reservation of any book

STRATEGIC PLAN FOR USING SOCIAL MEDIA

Proper planning should be necessary to implement any technology in any field whether it is library, institution, and Government organization etc.

1. Identify goals : Set the goal of library and Institution and make library as important as centers of culture and history of the cities and academic institutions.

2. Identify Ideal users : This service means to attract new users and retain existing members.

3. Allocate budget : Some networks are provided through paid services. So it should be necessary to check the budget for this.

4. Type of information : What type of information

will be provided, at what time and how it will be provided, and from where it can be provided?

5. Choose for the right Open Source Software : To provide the social networking in your library, you should be necessary to select multipurpose software in cost effective manner.

6. Choose your social networks : As there are many networks, select the most used network for library.

USE THE APPLICATION OF SOCIAL MEDIA WITH KOHA

1. Facebook : Facebook is a great tool to interact with users and it gives the library the right platforms to create and disseminate content. They can share any book with others through Facebook. Opinion of users about any book, review of book and likes and dislikes about the book may be read. New events and news, about any programme can be shared.

2. Twitter : Twitter is real-time connection, which creates an effective environment for dissemination of scholarly news and updates. It uses to elicit instant feedback and chat. To increase the reading habit and right use of time, library can give the list of books on particular topic.

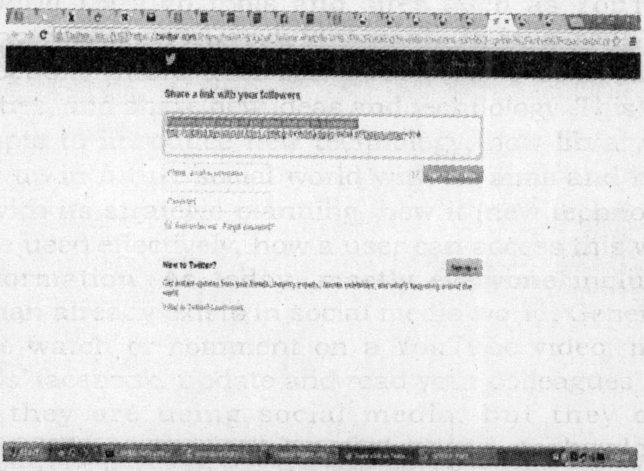

3. Delicious : User can bookmark any book, and could see what others have bookmarked. We can publish paper on recent trends.

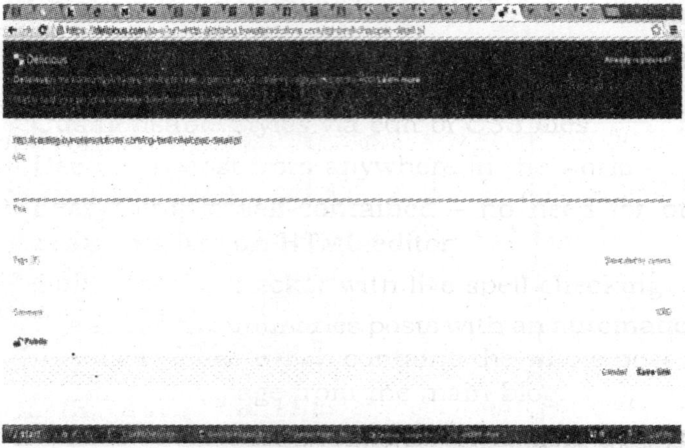

4. LinkedIn : A network of some libraries can be developed and communicate with each other. Libraries related various problems and services can be discussed. Valuable ideas can be transferred. Reviews on any book can be collected by sending the cover image of book. This is bridging the gap over the different libraries.

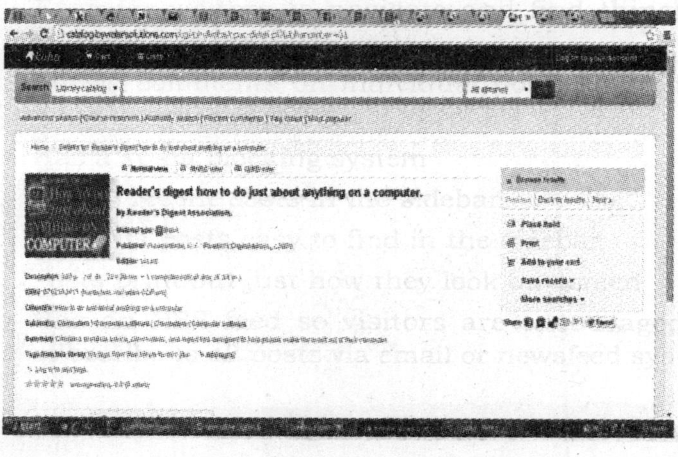

5. Tagging : It enables users to create subject heading keywords for the object at hand. It allows users to add and change not only content, but content describing content. In KOHA, users can tag library's collection with their own keywords and by thisactivity;user participates in the cataloguing process. They can see the tags given by others.

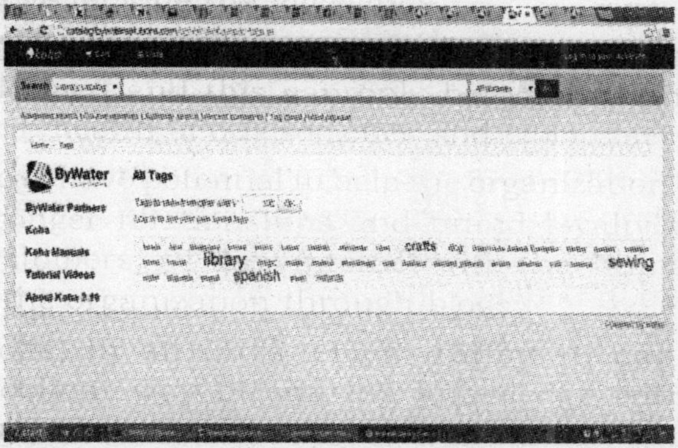

6. Mashups : The integration of some services in one place is called mashups. KOHA includes many services as combination of tagging, RSS, and integration of catalogues in other people, virtual shelves, comments or review to any books.

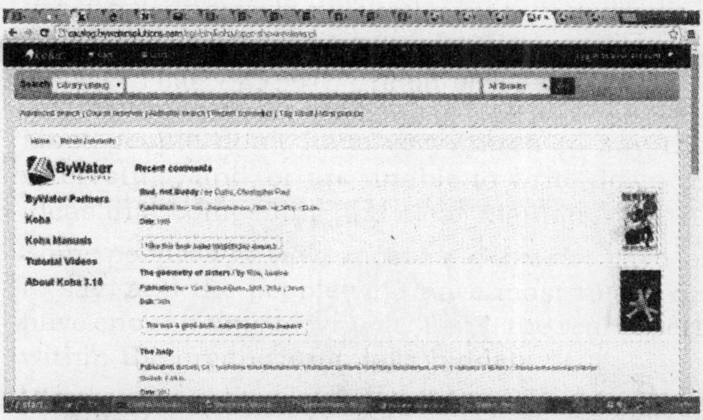

7. RSS : Recent collection in the library, List of any subject, bookmarked books can be subscribed through

RSS in KOHA. Current Awareness Service can be provided. In KOHA, go to system preferences, than OPAC and then type OPAC URL in OPACbaseURL. This allows users and librarians to subscribe to their searches and receive alerts when a new item is added to the collection. This means that every time a new item is added to the collection that matches your search terms your feed will be updated.

8. Instant Messaging : It allows to real-time text communication between users. By this, certain user seeking behaviors are easily detected and allow file sharing, co-browsing, etc. To receive updates via instant messenger of your choice, you can sign up with a service such as notify.me (*http://notify.me/*). It develops collaboration between librarians and users.

9. My Book Bag : Users can email or print the list of their choice, which is selected or found in the library catalog. This CART can be emptied by the user at any time. It's an invaluable tool for the educators and students. User can create a good self-bibliographic record and email to themselves or others for saving the time of searching.To send items by email from the cart: 'Select All' items in the Cart OR check boxes next to specific items you want to send by email, now Click 'Send' or to email cart: Enter an 'E-mail Address' and add a comment if you wish and Click 'Send'. User can place the order of hold for any book by this facility.

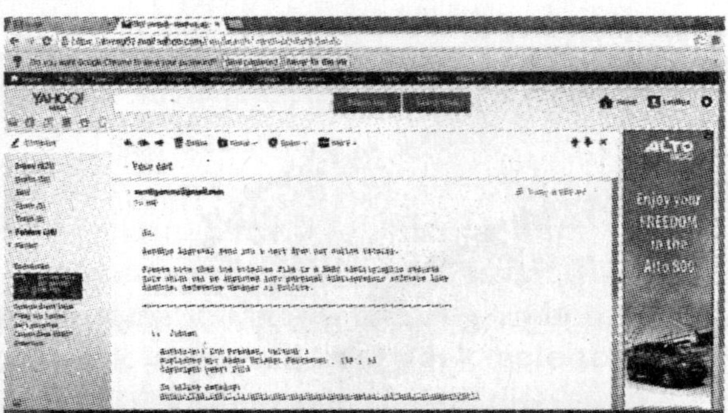

10. Virtual Shelves : Koha 'Lists' (previously known as 'Virtual Shelves') enable staff and patrons to create permanent booklists which can be shared with others. All items in a 'List' link directly to your library's catalog. To enable lists, the virtualshelves preference must be turned on. You can create online Reading Lists for users, as by age, on women, Mahatma Gandhi, and JawaharLal Nehru or perhaps something like 'Newberry Winners' or 'Oprah Club Books', create lists of 'Favorites', enable your community of users to contribute to readers' advisory by creating their own lists and sharing them with the public Lists come in three varieties:

1. ***Private* :** Which are able to be viewed and edited by the creator, but not by the public.
2. ***Public* :** These are viewed by all, but edited only by the list's creator.
3. ***Open* :** It can be viewed by all and edited by all (logging in is not necessary). Open Lists will appear under the Public Lists heading on the OPAC.

11. Review of Books : Manage and add comments and reviews via the OPAC. Comments are notes that can be passed by visitors to the OPAC. Comments may also be referred as reviews. The reviews on system preference must be set to ON for this feature to show in the OPAC. Comments can be added from the detailed view of any record in the catalog. To write a comment: Click the 'Comments' tab

12. Purchase Suggestions : Patrons can make suggestions to the acquisitions department regarding titles for the library. When patrons are logged into the OPAC they have the option to make purchase suggestions for items they cannot find in the library catalog. Any user can see the suggestion with their name.

13. Reservation of Books : User can place hold for issued book if it has issued. When the book is deposited, it will be issued to the first reserved.

14. Self-Renewable of Books : Book can be renewed at anytime and anywhere without visiting the library.

15. Network : A network or group of some libraries can be developed and users can see all collection of each library, union catalogue, and know the status. Besides, It can also be possible to transfer the book from any library.

KOHA : CHALLENGES AND OPPORTUNITIES

Not everyone is in agreement regarding the benefits of using social media. Some believe that there are barriers that prevent the use of social media in organizations, such as the perception of social media as a triviality, perceptions that social media is a waste of employee's work time, security issues, or lack of understanding of social media (Bradley & McDonald, 2011; Golden, 2011). The switch from in-house systems to a web-based open source library system is a great advance for GWAHS, but is not entirely trouble free. Some of these issues are common to web-based delivery of systems, and some relate specifically to Koha:

- Web-based systems need good web access to provide optimum benefits.
- OPAC times in Koha seem to be largely acceptable, but Cataloguing and Administration modes are often difficult to use if the internet connection is running slowly (a typical problem for rural and remote services).
- Broadband coverage in rural areas remains patchy. Slow speed and narrow bandwidth remain problems for service providers.
- The MARC cataloguing interface is not familiar to all librarians and the original cataloguing interface is somewhat laborious. However copy cataloguing is simplified with its Z39.50 interfaces

- Libraries face impatience from their organizations for transition to new and open methods for information service delivery, while facing the need to meet the challenge of professional development of library staff to familiarize with these new technologies.
- In rural areas, the information technology infrastructure and expertise of computer support staff to implement new technology is often inadequate to keep up with the pace of new developments.

CONCLUSION

There are some challenges in using social media, but its usage connects the people of remote areas. Social media facilitates communication among users and organizations using user-centered, participatory online technologies. With connection of KOHA, it provides a greatly enhanced library service in a very cost-effective manner, especially to those users in isolated locations who are rarely in a situation to visit the library personally. This method enables small libraries to establish a web presence.

REFERENCES

- Abram, Stephen and Sirsi, Dynix, 2006. One source, "Web 2.0, Library 2.0, and Librarian 2.0: preparing for the 2.0 world", vol. 2,no. 1, Also accessed on *http://www.imakenews.com/sirs/e_article000505688.cfm*
- Arora, Jagdish, 2009. "Web 2.0 and Library 2.0 innovative technologies for building libraries of tomorrow with examples of their applications at the INFLIBNET Centre". *Library herald,* vol. 47,no. 3, September 2009
- Balnaves, Edmund and Keast, Don, "Open source systems bring Web 2.0 to special libraries"
- *http://en.wikipedia.org/wiki/web_2.0*
- *http://www.w3schools.com/rss-simply-explained*
- *http://www.kohawikis.org*

- *http://192.168.1.2:8081*
- *http://www.watersolution.org*
- Rehman, Ataur and Shafique, Farzana, 2011. "Use of Web 2.0 and its implications for Libraries: perceptions of information professionals in Pakistan". *Library Philosophy and Practice.*
- Vimal Kumar V and Jassimudeen S, 2012. "Adoption and user perception of Koha library management system in India". *Annals of Library and Information Studies.* v 59, December 2012, pp 223-230

3

Usage of E-Resources from Academic Libraries to Social Media

Jagjit Singh
Librarian, Doaba College, Tanda Road,
Jalandhar City-144004 (Punjab)

ABSTRACT

Academic libraries are playing very important role in the field of academic and research activities. In ICT environment role of libraries is much increasing than routine functioning. ICT has changed lot of works of the libraries. It is more beneficial for human as well as libraries, now libraries work are moving fast and accurate than manual works. This paper explains how ICT is useful for libraries in a scientific way. ICT has great impact on libraries in term of organising, stored, dissemination and other ways in teaching and research.

Keywords : E-Resources, E-Books, E-Journals, ICT, Internet.

INTRODUCTION

Libraries are organizing information in every aspect at the world level; if information is organising manually then lot of difficulties can be arisen, but use of ICT in libraries has changed the functioning of the libraries at the global level. E-resources are very dynamic and easily available throughout the world. ICT is main source to deliver e-resources to academic libraries. Internet is also playing very active role to store, organize and dissemination information in the academic libraries. ICT savvy person can easily handle all e-resources available through the Internet. E-Resources collection is selected very carefully in view of expansive, quality, usability for academic libraries.

E-RESOURCES IN ICT ENVIRONMENT

Academic libraries are mainly dealing with gathering, stored, organized, accessibility, retrieval, and dissemination of information. ICT has changed the way of academic libraries with handing above functioning; now all steps are adopted by ICT in academic libraries. In modern era, ICT dramatically changed the all functioning of the academic libraries. Now academic libraries are commonly using e-book, e-journals, e-thesis, e-newspaper, e-mail, etc. Now academic libraries are providing following e-resources for their users.

- E-books
- E-journals
- E-newspapers
- Online Databases
- Abstracting and indexing database
- E-mail
- E-reports
- E-content
- E-thesis
- E-dissertation
- CD-Rom

WHY E-RESOURCES REQUIRED IN ACADEMIC LIBRARIES

E-Resources provide access to literally thousands of magazines and newspapers.

- E-Resources include publication subscriptions dating back the last 10 years (or more).
- E-Resources to find articles on a particular subject from many different publications at the same time without having to search each publication separately
- They are especially useful for finding information not yet available in books, or obtaining up-to-date information on current events or issues.
- E-Resources provide us with authoritative, accurate, current, objective reference material not readily available through a search engine like Google (more on this later...).
- E-Resources are free to library users, and can be accessed from any computer with Internet access, 24 hours a day, 7 days a week.

ADVANTAGES OF E-RESOURCES

Accessible : can be accessed from any computer on campus and usually any computer off campus, any time of the day or night, so there is no need to make a trip to the library

Easily searchable : each journal can be searched quick and easy often through the complete full text of articles and via online index

Speed : Articles/issues appear online before printed version is available

Interactive : Rapid turnaround time means articles can be read, commented by the readers, amended quickly and greater feedback thru the web

Links : Hypertext format should be exploited and links to related articles, information on other web sites, stable URLs for individual articles and email alerts when latest issue loaded.

Added Value : Advantages taken on the web is to

add value by using animation, virtual reality and interactive mathematical charts.

Inexpensive : savings can be made over printing costs, distribution costs and extra costs by new features.

Flexibility : E-journals evolved quickly. They are not tied to a format, printer, and distribution network

DISADVANTAGES OF E-RESOURCES

- Difficulty reading computer screens:
- limitations of computer monitor
- read information in the screen
- Often not included in indexing and abstracting services
- Search engines ignores PDF files
- Format that a large proportion of e-journal use

OBJECTIVES OF E-RESOURCES

- To create awareness among the users to the use of e-resources available the library
- To explore among library users how they can access relevant information on the internet
- To utilize users attention towards the use of e-resources available in the library
- To create healthy relation among the library staff and the users
- To promote research with the use of ICT to access e-resources

SOURCE OF E-RESOURCES

ICT is able to manage e-resource for the maximum use of their users. Academic libraries must store, organize and disseminate all e-resources to their users through ICT. All e-resources may be used properly if they follow proper attention of the users.

E-JOURNALS ACCESSIBILITY

- (*http://www.proquest.co.uk/en-UK/*)
- (*http://dl.acm.org/*)
- (*http://www.pubs.asce.org/journals/jrns.html*)
- (*http://www.asme.org/pubs/journals/*)
- (*www.astm.org/digitallibrary*)
- (*http://www.capitaline.com/intranet/INDEST-AICTE-AICTE_consortium.htm*)
- (*http://www.crisil.com/*)
- (*http://www.ebscohost.com*)
- (*http://www.sciencedirect.com/*)
- (*http://www.emeraldinsight.com/*)
- (*http://www.gmid.euromonitor.com*)
- (*http://www.atypon-link.com/action/show Publisher Journals?code=ITELF*)
- (*http://ieeexplore.ieee.org/*)
- *http://www.ieee.org/publications_standards/publications/subscriptions/prod/aspp_overview.html*)
- (*http://www.ietdl.org/*)
- (*http://www.insight.religaretechnova.com/*)
- (*http://www.nature.com/*)
- (*http://www.il.proquest.com/pqdauto*)
- (*http://www.opticsinfobase.org/*)
- (*www.interscience.wiley.com*)
- (*http://isiknowledge.com*)

E-BOOKS ACCESSIBILITY

- (*http://www.accessengineeringlibrary.com/*)
- (*http://www.springerlink.com/*)
- (*http://www.ei.org/ev2/home*)
- (*http://www.scopus.com/home.url*)

- Ebrary
- Oxford Scholarship
- Net Library

CONSORTIA IN INDIA

- CSIR (*http://www.niscair.res.in/ActivitiesandServices/MajorProjects/ majproj.htm#* ejournalcons)
- INDEST (http ://pani it. i itd.ac.in/indest)
- FORSA (*http://www.iiap.res.in/library/forsa.html*)
- IIM Consortia
- ICICI Knowledge Park (http://www. ici c knowledgepark.com/)
- ICMR (*http://vvww.jecccmr.informindia.co.in/about/about.asp*)
- ISRO
- HELINET (http ://j gateelinet. informindia. co. in/about/about.asp)
- UGC-INFONET (http://web. inflibnet.ac.in/infohigcinfonet/ugcinfonet.j sp)

CONCLUSION

At the end we can conclude that e-resources are becoming important source of any academic library. E-Resources are providing quick, relevant, and authentic information for their user. Academic libraries providing lot of resources for their users but in the absence of e-resources any academic library cannot be considered resourceful.

REFERENCES

1. http:// *www.education.com/* accessed on 20.11.2014
2. http:// *www.elernig-india.com/* accessed on 20.11.2014
3. http:// *www.ilias.de* accessed on 20.11.2014
4. Prakash, B.B., 2004. Impact of communication technology

on libraries and information services. *SERELS Journal of Information Management,* vol.41, pp.187-192.

5. Radjagopal, V., Chinnasamy, K. And Sudha, K., 2014. Role of ICt in e-resources of academic libraries, *CDICT,* pp.73-77.
6. Rao,Siriginidi Subba., 2005. Electronic books: their integration into library and information centers. *Electronic Library,* vol. 23 no.1
7. Singh, P.P and Sandhir Sharma., 2005. E-learning :new trends and innovations, New Delhi: Deep and Deep Publications.

4

Use of Social Networking in Libraries as Tool for Information Sharing and Services

Rajeev Manhas
University Librarian, Baba Farid University of Health Sciences, Faridkot – 151 203, Punjab, India

Asha
Coordinator, Centre for E-learning in Nursing Sciences, State Institute of Nursing & Paramedical Sciences, Badal, Punjab, India

Sapna Rani
Librarian, Baba Farid Law College, Faridkot, Punjab, India

ABSTRACT

Today world is shrinking socially more in virtual environment and it is very easy for the people to create, share or exchange information, ideas and other their day-to-day activities related pictures/ videos among the virtual communities and networks. This chapter depicts an overview of social media and its use in libraries as tool for information sharing and to provide information services. This chapter also highlights the *impact of social media* on information consumers, librarians and libraries. It will be a helping guide to users to make use the most of social media tool and avoid potential pitfalls. It also suggests the implications appropriate for global level practice based on available published guidance.

Keywords : Social Media; Social Networking; Information Services; Information Sharing; Libraries

INTRODUCTION

The popularity of the Internet has led to increased usage of social media networking sites, which are becoming an integral part of information sharing and communication among the various stakeholders (Jefferson University Experience, 2011). The results of survey conducted by the Neilsen Media Group indicated that social networks and blogs accounted for one in every four and a half minutes people spent online worldwide (Wire, 2010). It also highlights that, people throughout the world spend a staggering 110 billion minutes on social network sites and 75% of all people visit social media sites (even if they are not members) (Local Relationship Management, 2010). Indeed, the popularity of social networking is highly demonstrable by the number of people using those (Cheung, Chiu & Lee 2010). The applications of social media have been used globally as a communication tool. Social media is gaining popularity among the library & information science professionals and are actively utilizing its potential to enhance information sharing and to improve information services. Thus, there are a number of successful initiatives led by library & information sciences professionals. But, there are number of potential risks involved in use of social media due to its open accessibility. On the other hand, the increasing usage trend of these networking technologies have compelled libraries to include this tool in their conveys.

DEFINITION OF SOCIAL NETWORKING

According to Computing Dictionary (Social Network, 2011) social networking site as any website designed to allow multiple users to publish content of them. The information may be on any subject and may be for consumption by friends, mates, employers, employees just to mention a few.

Powell (2009) defines social networking as a community in which individuals are somehow connected through friendship, values, working relationships, idea and so on.

Seufert et al (1999) defines social networking in terms of knowledge networking as signifying a number of people, resources and relationships among them, who are assembled in order to accumulate and use knowledge primarily by means of knowledge creation and transfer processes, for the purpose of creating value. The concept of social networking is one of the tools of Web 2.0, which also forms the basis of library 2.0.

It can be inferred from above said definitions that the term social networking can be referred to as a web platform where various types of people and professionals can connect and interact with each other.

CLASSIFICATION OF SOCIAL MEDIA

According to Wikipedia, "social-media technologies can be of many different types like magazines, *Internet forums, weblogs, social blogs, micro blogging, wikis, social networks, podcasts,* photographs or pictures, video, rating and *social bookmarking.* Technologies include blogging, picture-sharing, *blogs,* wall-posting, music-sharing, *crowd sourcing* and *voice over IP,* to name a few (Social Media, 2014).

Kaplan and Haenlein (Kaplan & Michael 2010) divided the social media mainly into six different types as given below:

1. *Collaborative projects* (e.g. *Wikipedia*)
2. Blogs and microblogs (e.g. *Twitter* and *Tumblr*)
3. Content communities (e.g. *You Tube* and *Daily Motion*)

4. Social networking sites (e.g. *Facebook*)
5. Virtual game-worlds (e.g. *World of Warcraft*)
6. Virtual social worlds (e.g. *Second Life*)

SOCIAL NETWORKING IN LIBRARIES

The library is an organization, which collect information resources with the specific purpose of obtaining, preserving and making them available to their users. The efficiency and effectiveness of the library as a tool of Research and Learning is determined by the success of providing relevant and timely information to their users. Previously, the success of any library was measured on the basis of their traditional services, completeness and balance of collection. In recent times, the focus has changed towards technology driven delivery of information services. O'Brien (1996) and Dadzie (2007) emphasized that information must have the following qualities, so that it can be maximum utilized: relevance, accuracy, timeliness, currency, completeness, clarity and cost effectiveness. The traditional library system and its structures are proving unsatisfactory to respond quickly enough to technology driven environment. However, change is not desirable but also mandatory as technology has much potential that cannot be ignored. The biggest change in today's patrons from those in the past is their intense reliance on technology such as cell phones, computers, and access to the Internet etc (Ayiah, 2014).

Libraries and other business organizations are using social networking platform to interact and reach out to their clients. This platform has been embraced by libraries in their service delivery even though resources available to them abound. Students also use this platform to share information amongst themselves on any subject and topic. The use of these tools has been affirmed by Bell (2007) that Academic libraries do not only use social media for communication purposes, but had adapted their research strategies to this environment.

Yale Science Libraries, Adelphi University Libraries, Carnegie Mellon University Libraries, Cambridge University Library and Norwegian University of Science and Technology Library are just a few examples of the International University Libraries with social networking websites.

The social media websites are mostly used to (Ayiah, 2014):

1. announcement of the library programmes
2. give students the opportunity to ask questions related to the use of the library
3. teach basic searching tools
4. paste new books on the social media website to inform the library community
5. send information about updates to clients
6. ask a Librarian

Academic Libraries in India can also respond to the needs of modern day patrons by applying efficient technologies such as social networking, mobile application, and online check in/check outs to their information service delivery.

These developments in the operations of library service delivery should encourage Indian libraries to reinvent itself to respond adequately to this call by investing in technologies that have direct effect on the operations and information delivery service of the library. To achieve this, Indian libraries must upgrade library staff skills in information Technology (IT) so as to be able to understand and use Social Networking sites to their maximum (Ayiah, 2014).

BENEFITS OF SOCIAL NETWORKING SITES TO LIBRARIES

Social networking sites have its own advantages to Librarians and Clients. Some of the benefits are as follows (Ayiah, 2014):

- Social networking sites will facilitate collaborations and promote effective communication between Librarians and their clients.
- It will generate a flow of information excluded from search engines and Library Catalogues.
- Social networking sites will lead future delivery of information to meet search queries
- The crucial aim of librarians is to make library resources available to clients so if social networking sites will help achieve this goal then it should be pursued vigorously.
- Social networking sites wall linked to a library's web page has the potential of reaping great results by attracting and serving Distance Education Students. Watts, Dodds & Newman (2002) stress that it is through social networking sites that any person is capable of communicating and delivering a message to a distant target person.
- It will help Librarians and Libraries to keep pace with technologies and compete effectively with the developed World.

RECOMMENDATIONS

The following recommendations are suggested for adoption in an effort to improve library services by librarians to patrons (Ayiah, 2014):

- It is advocate that librarians should formulate policies on the use of social networking sites and adaptation it in the library environment. Such a policy should be designed in a way to include: a designated member of staff at a senior management level, with appropriate professional qualifications, to be responsible for the planning, implementation, operation and monitoring of services of the social network site of the library.
- Expertise should be sought from libraries of other

countries who have implemented these technologies for assistance in the design for the Indian Libraries.

- Periodic evaluation of the social networking sites should be carried out to determine areas requiring attention. Evaluation is important because it helps to match objectives of the social networking sites with performance.

CONCLUSION AND SOCIAL MEDIA GUIDELINES FOR PROFESSIONALS

Electronic communication has altered the way we interact with one another, organizations, and products. The use of social media technologies can be helpful tool for the librarians and their clients but these technologies have both advantages and disadvantages also. It is suggested that these technologies be used and adopted carefully and social ethics should be taken care before adoption. Today's student is not interested in printed work in most of the cases; for librarians to make libraries interesting innovations such as social networking site should be introduced to attract them to the library environment. Social networking sites will work to establish a cordial relationship between librarians and clients; market the library's services; announce library programmes on the social media website and so on. These kinds of technologies provide the libraries an enabling platform that goes beyond the traditional service delivery and allow library clients to interact in real time with librarians in the comfort of their homes. Librarians must acquire the necessary skills in information technology to meet the challenging demands of social networking sites (Ayiah, 2014).

The ever-changing digital landscape can bring uncertainty to professionals when it comes to appropriate online conduct. The tips below are guidelines on how to create a constructive, effective, and authentic online interactive platform of information sharing and dissemination whether on Facebook, Twitter, LinkedIn YouTube, or any other social channel (Social Media Guidelines, 2014).

1. Build your brand : The information provided on the social website should be authentic and in proper manner, so that the brand value of organization be there.

2. Transparency : Identify yourself, write in the first person, and don't be afraid to show your personality. Own your voice. Social media is all about continuous dialogue. Be smart, post smarter.

3. Honesty : Do not make false or misleading comments/statements. If you make a mistake, take responsibility for it. It's ok! It's better to own it and clarify than to deny or ignore and open yourself to further criticism.

4. Respectfulness : Exercise discretion and confidentiality when referring to others, including coworkers and clients.

5. Add value : Stick to what you know. Post meaningful comments, and aim for quality. Interested in gaining new knowledge? Ask! Someone will likely post back to you!

6. Be diligent : Check your sources. Separate opinions from facts. Know the difference between offering suggestions and offering advice. Offering advice could lead to liability.

7. Stay engaged : Stay informed, post regularly, and respond to comments in a timely manner.

REFERENCES

Ayiah, Efua Mansa, 2014. Social Networking: a tool to use for effective service delivery to clients by African Libraries. Retrieved from the website: *http://conference.ifla.org/past-wlic/2011/183-ayiah-en.pdf*

Bell, S.J., 2007. Building better academic libraries with Web 2.0 technology tools. *Library Issues*, vol.*28*,*no*.2.pp.1–4.

Cheung, C.M.K., Chiu, P.Y. and Lee, M.K.O. (2010). *Online social networks: Why do students use Facebook?. Computers in Human Behavior,* Article in Press.

Dadzie, Perpetua S., 2007. Information Literacy: assessing the readiness of Ghanaian Universities. *Information Development, vol.23.no.*4, pp.265-277.

Kaplan, Andreas M and Michael, Haenlein, 2010. Users of the world, unite! The challenges and opportunities of social media. *Business Horizons,* vol.*53no.*1,pp.61.

Local Relationship Management, 2010. *The Value of Social Media to the Fitness and Leisure Industry.* Retrieved from the Local Relationship Management website: *http://www.stevejack.com/downloads/special%20reports/SPE CIAL%20REPORT%20Value% 20of%20Social%20Media%20to% 20the% 20Fitness%20and%20Leisure%20Industry.pdf*

O'Brien, J., 1996. *Management information systems: managing information technology in the networked enterprise.*

Powell, Juliette, 2009. "33 million People in the Room: how to create, influence, and run a successful Business with Social networking. Pearson Education, Inc" *https://idv.sagapub.com/cgi/content/abstract/23/4/266*

Seufert, Andreas, Krogh Georg, Von and Andrea, Bach, 1999. "Towards knowledge networking". *Journal of Knowledge Management.* Vol. 3. No. 3. Pp.180-190.

Social Media. Retrieved from the *http://en.wikipedia.org/wiki/Social_media* (Accessed on 2 December 2014)

Social Media Guidelines for Nurses, 2014. Retrieved from the *http://rnao.ca/ news/socialmediaguideline*

Social Network. 2011. *The Free On-line Dictionary of Computing.* Retrieved June 23, 2011, from Dictionary.com Retrieved from the website: http://dictionary.reference.com/browse/social network

The use of social media by graduate health science students: The Thomas Jefferson University experience, 2011. *Health Policy Newsletter,* vol. *24,no.*3.

Watts, D. J., Dodds, P.S. & Newman, M.E.J. 2002. Identity and search in social networks. *Science,* vol.*296,no.*5571, 1302.

Wire, Neilsen. (2010). *Social networks/blogs now accounts for one in every four and a half minutes online.* Retrieved from *http://blog.nielsen.com/nielsenwire/global/social-media-accounts-for-22-percent-of-time-online/.*

5

How Social Media is Currently Used by Librarians

R S Aswal
Librarian CDAC, Noida

INTRODUCTION

The usage of social media by library community was little relevance but in recent years it is widely used to fulfill a variety of objectives. It is very potential tools to facilitate much closer relationships between libraries and their patrons to deliver customer services and resources. It is a powerful communication tools to interact with faculty, staff, and students in new ways.

OBJECTIVES OF SOCIAL MEDIA

Libraries use social media to fulfill several objectives, with most focused on promotion (visibility for and usage of the library service and resources), which can be summarized as follows:

- To seek suggestions on the library and its services for self-evaluation purposes, enquiries and feedback;
- To reach library users in their homes or 'virtual spaces' as today's modern online library is no longer

solely relying on its physical space as an access point;

- To promote events, library services, new acquisitions;
- To encourage collaboration, for example through collection development and building repositories of collaborative content specific to certain user groups;
- To increase usage of library collections by promoting new and existing content;
- To connect with other librarians and keep abreast of industry news;
- To build a sense of community with both users and also with other institutions and industry contacts;
- To connect with new students joining the university;
- To highlight subject specific information;
- To promote new additions;
- To publish or link to pictures;
- As teaching tool to promote information literacy, technology and writing tips.

ADVANTAGES OF USING SOCIAL MEDIA

Advantages for librarians and libraries when using social media are seen to be:

- Financially the costs of using social media are perceived to be low;
- It requires little training;
- It promotes library services and disseminates news quickly, delivering this information more directly to library users;
- It increases engagement and interactions with library users;
- It helps gather feedback to enhance user services;
- The promotion of library holdings via social media can help increase usage of content;

- It enhances communication both within the library and with other departments;
- It can be used for outreach activities through onward sharing, well beyond the institution itself, helping build connections and reputation more broadly.

CHALLENGES OF USING SOCIAL MEDIA

Challenges associated with using social media in libraries include the following:

- Social media can require considerable time commitment from library staff;
- Social media can require technological expertise, for example customizing applications to provide access to online catalogs;
- It can be a challenge for librarians to use an informal but presentable tone, or deliver social media content in a bilingual or multilingual region;
- Levels of interest in and skills with using social media vary enormously across library staff;
- There are limited funds to support more advanced social media usage/features and the training that would be required to enable this;
- A library needs to work hard to maintain engagement with library users and attract popularity (followers, likes and so on);
- It can be difficult to maintain library branding for content/resources made accessible via social media;
- There are potential copyright issues when using social media such as YouTube to build collections;
- External factors such as Internet connectivity, technological infrastructure and government restrictions on the use of social media may restrict access.

CHANNELS OF SOCIAL MEDIA

Popular social media channels are:

Twitter	• Distribute library news and information • Provide customer service to library patrons • Build connections with researchers • Build connections with other librarians and institutions
Facebook	• Distribute library news and information • More social and less formal than Twitter - share photographs and run competitions • Arrange events including tracking RSVPs and sending event updates • Engagement with students
YouTube	• Steaming film collections • Instructional 'how to' videos teaching information literacy skills and how to use library services and resources
Pinterest	• Promote general library collections, digital and archive special collections and information literacy • Set up of online repositories for students to pin researched references as part of collaborative group work • Display book titles to save time browsing and promote new titles • Provide an arena for students and course leaders to pin reviewed and recommended reading for a particular topic • Develop communities with other online libraries
Blogs	• Blogs are used for sharing information and news.

Twitter and Facebook as the most used social media tools in libraries.There are also a number of other social media products that are being used by librarians that reflect regional preferences and the need for the specific functions offered by niche applications.

HOW TO PROMOTE LIBRARY SOCIAL MEDIA CHANNELS

The most popular way of promoting library social media channels currently is through links from the library website, followed by email signatures. Cross-promotion of social media services was also frequently used, (e.g. across other library and institutional channels) with links to Twitter from a library social bookmarking.

THE FUTURE FOR SOCIAL MEDIA IN THE LIBRARY

The shift of provision of library resources online has also brought about a huge shift in the role of the librarian – with this role becoming more integrated into the user communities within the institution. Feedback in our focus groups and interviews indicated that social media is seen as an important support tool for transitioning into this new role.

Some librarians see their role becoming one of helping users find paths through complex content, and directing them towards making useful connections as efficiently as possible – potentially by merging smart applications and human crowdsourcing, with the smart component drawing on the human element by using social sources to retrieve information that is personalized and relevant to a specific user. Some librarians highlight the value which can be added by providing a human element to complex content; providing a guide to users enabling them to make fast connections between multiple channels and information sources.

CONCLUSIONS

Most librarians feel strongly positive about the potential for social media to help increase engagement between users and library staff and services. Social media is also seen as an effective outreach tool, helping librarians promote the work of their faculty and connect more deeply with the broader library community.

6

Social Media and Library Service

Bibhash Kumar Mishra
Assistant Librarian, Kumaun University
S S J Campus, Almora (Uttarakhand)

ABSTRACT

The paper provides basic information regarding social media and social networking. The 4 libraries use blogs as an information tool. In the present scenario social networking sites are well accepted among the professionals for the dissemination of information. Social networks are the most promising and embracing technology. Paper also provides information about web 2.0.

Keywords : Social Media, Social Networking, Web 2.0, library 2.0, Facebook.

INTRODUCTION

"The social networking can prove to be the boon for libraries disseminating the information to its registered as well as non-registered (large audience) members. Social media should be considered to be the part of edutainment. In the present electronic environment, the needs of the users are changing day by day and to fulfill the information requirement of the users' community, library professionals need to upgrade their tools and techniques. The information has to be provided in a better and efficient way, so that the information requirement of the users can be fulfilled in a better way. LIS professionals are adopting best methods in the form of social media to cater the need of the end users. (Vikas Singh, 2013) "

WHAT IS WEB 2.0?

"The term Web 2.0 refers to the development of online services that encourage collaboration, communication and information sharing. It represents a shift from the passive experience of static "read only" web pages to the participatory experience of dynamic and interactive web pages. In other words, Web2.0 reflects changes in how we use the web rather than describing any technical or structural change.

Service Types	*Example*
Social Network	Facebook
Video and Photo Sharing	Youtube, Flickr
Blogging	Blogger, Wordpress
Microblogging	Twitter, Tumblr
Wikis	Peanut Butter, Tikiwiki
Resource Organisation	Page Flakes, Netvibes

Many Web2.0 services, such as the examples provided, are often referred to as "social media" due to their role in supporting communication and building online communities. (Khisanya, 2014)"

BLOGS AND WIKIS

"Blogs and wikis are fundamentally 2.0, and their global proliferation has enormous implications for libraries. Blogs may indeed be an even greater milestone in the history of publishing than web-pages. They enable the rapid production and consumption of Web-based publications. In some ways, the copying of printed material is to web-pages as the printing press is to blogs. Blogs are HTML for the masses.

A blog or weblog is a powerful two way web based tool. A blog is a website where library users can enter their thoughts, ideas, suggestions, and comments. Any library user can publish a blog post easily and cheaply through a web interface, create "What's New" for users, marketing of Information, user conversation about the services and resources, Post the meeting/conferences output, Place the discussion forum, and any reader can place a comment on a blog post. Wikis are essentially open web-pages, it is an online encyclopedia where any registered user can write, amend or otherwise edit articles in the library world well note. (Khisanya, 2014) "

SOCIAL NETWORKS

"Social networking could enable librarians and patrons not only to interact, but to share and change dynamically in an electronic medium. Users can create accounts with the library network. Social networks are perhaps the most promising and embracing technology discussed here. They enable messaging, blogging, streaming media, and tagging, discussed later. MySpace, FaceBook, Del.icio.us, Frappr, and Flickr are networks that have enjoyed massive popularity in Web 2.0. While MySpace and Facebook enable users to share themselves with one another (detailed profiles of users' lives and personalities), Del.icio.us enables users to share Web resources and Flickr enables the sharing of pictures. Frappr is a bit of a blended network, using maps, chat rooms, and pictures to connect individuals. (Khisanya, 2014)"

LIBRARY BLOGS

"The new information, materials, services, databases, etc. can be disseminate via blog. In the digital environment, to promote awareness of the library programs and services, blog is very useful tool to broadcast the information to end users due to its very fast and simple way to post content online. To create awareness amongst the users especially in the costly resources like online databases, the blog is very helpful tool. The users can be motivated to take advantage of library resources more frequently and more effectively by the library professions via blog. The thoughts, ideas and suggestions about the library resources and its services, can enter by the users through the library blogs and librarian can also know the user's views, ideas and thinking about library resources and services and its utility. A library blog entry might contain text, images or links to other blogs and web page. Any library user can publish a blog post easily and cheaply through a web interface, and reader can place a comment on a blog post. With the increase use of ICT in the library filed the use of blogs has been increasing day by day. (Lata, 2014)"

USE OF WEB 2.0 APPLICATIONS FOR LIBRARY SERVICES

"Web 2.0 technologies provide librarian and professional with new ways to engage students, and even allow student participation on a global level. Web 2.0, a term popularized by O'Reilly (2005). Libraries and librarians began to discuss Web 2.0 services and their relevance in library context soon after the term was coined in 2005. The concept of Library 2.0 is borrowed from web 2.0. Web 2.0 applications are being used in libraries. A range of purpose is presented here which describe use of Web 2.0 Applications:

- **P**osting resources reviews and information on new programs and books of internet, e.g. wikis and blogs.
- **W**ikis are used as an integral part of the curriculum development as a planning space to develop the unit.
- **S**haring of information becomes easier.
- **P**rofessional as well as users stay informed with what is happening with in department and colleagues.
- **C**ommunication with staff, student and professional

about upcoming g events become easier.

- Embedding codes into web pages and bookmarking relevant resources.
- It is user-centered. Users participate in the creation of the content and services they view within the library's web-presence, OPAC, etc.
- Encourage users to help build the information environment

Libraries can design attractive services using Web 2.0 applications without spending huge Budgets for online hosting and storage. (Sharma, 2013)"

Launch year of Major Social Network Sites

Sr.No.	*Launching Year*	*Major Social Network Sites*
1	1997	Six Degrees.com
2	1998	Live Journal Asian Avenue
3	1999	Black Planet, Lunar Storm (SNS relaunch)
4	2000	MiGente, Six Degree Closes
5	2001	Cyworld, Ryze, Fotolog
6	2002	Friendster, Skyblog, Couchsurfing, Linked In
7	2003	MySpace, Tribe.net, Open BC/Xing, Last FM, Orkut Dogster, Hi5, Multiply, aSmallWord, Flickr, Piczo, Mixi, Facebook (Harvard only), Dodgeball, care2 (SNS relaunch)
8	2004	Catster, Hyves, Yahoo!360, Youtube, Cyworld (China)
9	2005	Bebo(SNS relaunch), facebook (high scholar networks) Ning, Facebook (corporate networks), Windows live spaces
10	2006	Cyworld (U.S), Twitter, MyChurch, Facebook (everyone)

WHAT ARE THE USES AND APPLICATIONS OF SOCIAL NETWORKING IN THE LIBRARIES?

We can use the Social Networking services in the library by many ways such as

1) Marketing Library Services
2) Providing the link and information
3) Sharing-discussion topics pictures/Music/Video
4) Participation-create a dialog
5) Getting Feedback (Vaibhav Manohar, 2013)

CONCLUSION

"All together, the use of these technologies and applications, the library's collection will change, becoming more interactive and fully accessible. The library services will change, focusing more on the facilitation of information transfer and information literary rather than providing controlled access to it". (Brundaban Nahak, 2014). We can use social networking tools for enhancing library services for users. Library professionals should use new social networking tools to offer service to their user.

REFERENCE

Khisanya, S. K., 2014. Web 2.0, Library 2.0 Technology and Web 3.0. *From real to virtual: Transformation in Libraries.* New Delhi: Society for Information Research & Studies (SIRs). pp. 79-85

Lata, P., 2014. Blog: Auseful tool for disseminating the information. *From real to virtual: Transformation in Libraries.* New Delhi: Society for Information Research & Studies (SIRs). pp. 109-113

Sharma, S., 2013. Web2.0: In Present Scenario. *Knowledge Organization in Academic Libraries.* New Delhi: Viva Books. pp. 169-174

Vaibhav Manohar, S. R. (2013). Usefulness of Social Networking Tools for Modern Library Services. *Knowledge Organization in Academic Libraries.* New Delhi: Viva Books. pp. 393-399

Vikas Singh, G. G., 2013. Role of Social Media in Libraries for Information Dissemination. *Managing Information Resources in Digital Environment.* New Delhi: Society for Information Research & Studies (SIRs). pp. 240-246

7

Social Media Marketing

Gurpreet Kaur
Librarian, T.S.G.G.S. Khalsa College, Amritsar

ABSTRACT

This chapter discusses social media marketing or social networking as a new tool in information management. It explicates how social networking can enhance library outreach and librarian's collaboration. It presents social media as an instrument tomanage information that is capable of creating future prospects, opportunities and hope for library users and library professionals. The emergence of social media and subsequent trend of change in media consumption are pushing libraries to adopt social media as one of their marketing and public relation tools. This chapter also discuss why use social media market in the libraries and challenges of using social media in libraries. This chapter also discuss about the social media products and services such as twitter, face book, YouTube, bloggers and micro blogs, social news site etc.

INTRODUCTION

Social media has become an increasingly familiar tool employed in libraries to market services and resources to current and prospective patrons. The emergence of social media and subsequent trend of change in media consumption are pushing libraries to adopt social media as one of their marketing and public relation tools. Currently the development of internet and increased used of mobile devices such as smart phones , tablets have contributed greatly to the availability of various contents online , the contents previously used to be available only on the mainstream media outlets such as print media, radio and televisions. The social and communication pattern of our society are being shifted by the influx of social media products and services such as twitter, face book, YouTube, bloggers, word press etc.

Social Media : Social media is internet based tool for sharing and discussing information among human beings. Social media is all about networking and networking in a way that espouses trust among parties and communities involved. Any website which allows user s to share their contents opinions, views and encourages interactions and community building can be classified as a social media.It is difficult to give an explicit definition of the term social media. Many are confused with the use of term with others like social networking, social news, web 2.0, wikis etc let's simplifies the term by taking the words and reporting them into their different meaning.

Social : Social means pertaining to, devoted to or characterised by the friendly companionship or relations.

Media : Media means the communication such as radios, television, newspapers, magazines that reach people widely. So we can say that social media is a social instrument of communication. It can be called as strategy and outlet for broadcasting communication.

Safko and Brake (2009) observe that social media refers to activities, practices, behaviours among communities of the peoples who gather online to share information, knowledge and opinions using conversational media.

Weinberg (2009) notes that social media "relates to the sharing of information, experiences and perspectives through community oriented websites"

Social media are media for social interactions using highly accessible and reliable publishing techniques. Social media used web based technology to transform and broadcast media monologues into social media dialogues. They support the democratization of knowledge and information and transform people from content consumers to content producers (Wikipedia 2010)

Social Media Marketing : Social media is a form of internet marketingthat implement' various social media networks in order to achieve marketing communication and branding social goals. Social media marketing primarily covers activities involving social sharing of contents, videos and images for marketing purposes. Social media marketing is a new trend and rapidly growing in a way inwhich business are reaching out to targeted customers easily. Social media marketing can be simply defined as the use social media channels to promote and its products. This kind of marketing can be thought of as a subset of online marketing activities that complete traditional web based promotion strategies such as e-mail newsletters and online advertising campaign

Categories of social media marketing : The term social media is a broad one that encompasses a vast array of online resources. Since it is not possible to discuss all the different types of social media here, the following main categories were chosen:

1. **Social Networking Site :** First Social Networking site and social network are generic terms for sites that are used to connect users with similar background and interests. Most social networks have the same features, personal profile, the ability to add friends, photo albums and a variety of ways to interact with friends and their contents. A current example of social media isface book. It is the most popular social network. Face book users can find and add friends, find and follow companies, entertainers, politicians and more, create and share

photo albums, events in vitiation and basic blog packs create free page for a company business group, find and join group.

2. **Blog :** According to stoke the word 'Blog' was first coined by peter merholz in 1999.Paul Beelen describes blogs as web pages which can be easily updated, published by a single person or group of people, typically as brief articles displayed in reverse chronological order.

3. **Micro blog :** You may have heard of micro blog or micro blogging and wondered what the phrase meant. Twitter is the mostpopularmicro blogging site, one drive by the most textual messages or micro blogs. Twitter is the third most popular social network. It is used as place to report, to react to and engage topics of national and international import ranging from wars and natural disasters to elections and celebrity events. Twitter users can find and add more friends, adding friends is not a mutual relationship. They do not have to accept you as a friend for you to be able to follow them. Twitter user can find and follow company's entertainers, politicians. Twitter can store links to anything on the web.

4. **Social news site :** a social news site lets visitors submit and vote on contents. Socialnews Site serves as a filter that separates compelling contents from mundane contents on the web when users find content that interests that can submit the content to a social news site

5. **Social bookmarking site :** social bookmarking site is similar to a social news site, but the value presented to the users is focused on allowing them to collect and store interesting links they have found and may wish to reverse it. Users store organized contents from the web via links bookmarks.

6. **Media storing site :** a media storage site encompasses users to upload multimedia content, videos, images, podcast and other form of media. This segment of social media has become particularly influenced through video sharing sites such as YouTube, photo sharing sites such as flicker, presentation sites such as slide share.

ADVANTAGES OF SOCIAL MEDIA MARKETING

1. Cost related : The main advantage of Social media marketing is cost related. The financial barriers to Social media marketing are quite low compared to others. The majority of social media sites are free to access, create profit and post information.

2. Social Interaction : one of the most notable phenomena of new media is how it has increased and created new form of social interaction. People spend more than a quarter of their online involved in communication activities e.g. emails,IM Chat and social networks.

3. Interactivity : Interactivityis one of the defining characteristics of new media technology, giving greater access to information as well as supporting increased user control and engagement with social media content. Interactivity depends on the context. In an online social networking context, interactivity refers to usercentred interactivity with machines messages or other users.

4. Targeted market : Social media provide marketers with the ability to target audiences and consumers based on site user personal interests and what their friends like. For example, list country music as one of your interests on a social networking site; you will most likely be seeing ads about country music artists.

DISADVANTAGES OF SOCIAL MEDIA MARKETING

1. Time intensive : Social media is interactive and successful, two way exchanges take commitment. The nature of marketing changes in social networks with the focus placed on establishing long term relationship the first preliminary consideration and probably the most important is that social media marketing requires a significant time investment.

2. Trademark and copyright issues : it is the utmost importance for companies to protect their own trademarks and copyright when using social media to promote their brands andproducts, when using social media, whether via a third party outlet or a company's own social media platforms, marketers should regularly monitor the use of their trademarks and copyrights.

3. Trust, Privacy and Security Issues : Using Social media to promote one's brand, products or services can also implicit trust privacy and security issues. It is important for companies to aware of theirissues and takes appropriate measures to minimize their exposure to liability related to personal data collection use and maintenance.

4. User-Generated Content (UGC) : During the lastfew years, users have spent more time and shared more information, thoughts and opinions with each other easily via the internet. Also, new forms of content generations, communication and collaboration have come out on the Internet. Marketing strategies involving social networking sites or other social media incorporate users generate content into the field. For examples UGC allows Internet users to make comments in various forms, such as photos, videos, podcasts, reviews, article and blogs. UGC holdsmuch promise as a marketing tool. In addition, user generated content comes with a relatively high degree of credibility in the eyes of consumers, particularly if someone created the content for example or a tweet between friends.

5. Negative feedbacks : Social media, in a way, converts consumers into markets and advertisers and consumers can create positive or negative pressure for the company, its products and its services depending both on howthe company is presented online and on the quality of products and services presented to the customer.

Why use Social media market in the Libraries : Libraries have several objectives that they are using social media to help them achieve which can be summarized as follows:

1. To seek opinion on the library and its services for self- evaluation purposes, to encourage debate and to instigate an opportunity to rebound to library user feedback.
2. To publicize events, services, news and presence.
3. To encourage collaboration, for example through collection development and building repositories of collaborative content specific to certain user groups.
4. To increase usage of library collection by promoting news and existing content.
5. To connect with other libraries and keep abreast of industry news.

CHALLENGES ASSOCIATED WITH USING SOCIAL MEDIA IN LIBRARIES

Challenges associated with using social media in libraries include the following:

1. Social media can require considerable time commitment from library staff.
2. Social media can require technological expertise, for example customizing applications to provide access to online catalogues.
3. It can be a challenge for librarians to use an informal but presentable tone, or deliver social media content in a bilingual or multilingual region.
4. Levels of interest in and skills with using social media vary enormously across library staff.
5. There are limited funds to support more advanced social media usage/ features and the training that

would be required to enable this.

6. A library needs to work hard to maintain engagement with library users and attract popularity (followers, likes and so on).
7. It can be difficult to maintain library branding for content/resources made accessible via social media.
8. There are potential copyright issues when using social media such as YouTube to build collections.
9. External factors such as Internet connectivity, technological infrastructure and government restrictions on the use of social media may restrict access.

CONCLUSION

Social media can be established anywhere with an Internet connection and it should be considered b markets, advertisers and online content creators. Social media marketing began with an explanation of the social media phenomenon, accompanied with a definition of social media and reasons for consumer and corporate adoption of social media. The emergence of social media and subsequent trendof change in media consumption are pushing libraries to adopt social media as one of their marketing and public relation tools.

REFERENCE

- Ross, J. 2009, A corporate guide for social media. Retrieved from *http://www.forbes.com*
- Miller. Rohan, Social media and its implications for viral marketing, Asia Pacific Public Relations Journal, Vol.11
- Bruns, T.A, 2013, using Social media in Libraries: Best Practise edited by Charles Harmon and Michael Messina. Public services Quarterly, Vol.9,no.4,pp.313-314
- *http://www.queenslibrary.org*
- solis,B,2010, Defining Social media:2006-2010. Retrieved from *http://www.brainsolis.com*
- Evans, Dove, 2010, Social media marketing, Wiley publishing, Inc.
- http://www.socialmediamarketimg.com

8

Usage of Blogs in Libraries

Jagjit Singh

Librarian, Doaba College, Tanda Road,
Jalandhar City-144004 (Punjab)

ABSTRACT

A blog (also called a weblog or web log) is a website consisting of entries appearing in reverse chronological order with the most recent entry appearing first. Blogs typically include features such as comments and links to increase user interactivity. Blogs are created using specific publishing software. This paper discusses various aspects of blog, features, types, merit, demerit and their application in libraries.

1. INTRODUCTION

A blog is sometimes referred to as an online personal journal. It is a site designated for an individual to write about his/her daily experiences, to illicit thoughts and often allowing readers to offer their comments. The term is a shortened form of "weblog". Authoring a blog, maintaining a blog or adding content to an existing blog is referred to as "blogging". Individual articles on a blog are referred to as "blog posts", "posts", or "entries", and the person who created the blog post is often called a "blogger".

Variations of the term *blog*:

Blogging : The act of writing a post for a blog

Blogger : A person who writes content for a blog

Blogosphere : The online community of blogs and bloggers

There was a time when the Internet was just an informational tool. In the early life of the World Wide Web some 20 years ago, websites were simple and provided a one-sided conversation. As time went on, the Internet became more interactive with the introduction of transaction-based websites and online shopping, but the online world remained one-sided.That all changed with the evolution of Web 2.0 wherein user-generated content became an integral part of the online world. Today, users expect websites to provide a two-way conversation and web logs (or blogs) were born.

2. HISTORY OF BLOGS

The earliest blogs started in the late 1990s as online diaries. Individuals posted information on a daily basis about their lives and opinions. The daily posts were listed in reverse date order, so readers viewed the most recent post first and scrolled through previous posts. The format provided an ongoing inner monologue from the writer. As blogs evolved, interactive features were added to create a two-way conversation. Readers took advantage of features that allowed them to leave comments on blog posts or link to posts on other blogs and websites to further the dialogue. As the Internet has become more social, blogs have gained in popularity. Today, there are over 100 million blogs with more entering the blogosphere everyday. Blogs have become more than online diaries. In fact, blogging has become an important part of the online and offline worlds with popular bloggers impacting the worlds of politics, business and society with their words.

3. WHAT IS BLOGGING?

Each and every skill need to run and manage a Blog is called blogging. Blogging includes Skills Like Search Engine Optimization, Social Media Marketing, Writing, Editing and Publishing Posts, Designing and Maintaining the Design of your Website, etc. We need to learn every skill to be a Blogger like a good writer to write lot of Unique and Quality content for our website. He should be a good Search Engine Optimizer to Optimize his blog according to rules and regulations set by Search engines. We Need to be a Social Media Marketer and Optimizer to influence our websites or blogs with social media Power which is very strong these days. It is true that we can hire Experts or freelancers for each job but we will need a lot of money for doing that, so rely on self and learn each and every skill slowly so that for becoming a Good Blogger.

4. KEY FEATURES OF A BLOG FOR OWNERS

- Allows multiple user logins
- Easy for users to write and upload posts and edit them later if needed
- Allows users to save drafts prior to final posting – so a post doesn't have to be completed in one go
- Easy for users to embed images and videos and provide optimised alt text
- Allows full coding rather than just plain text so that posts can have hyperlinks to other pages in the main website or to other posts, or to another website or blog, etc
- Looks and works the same in all popular browsers
- All posts mentioned in the sitemap.xml ...
- SEO optimisation allowing customisation of <titles> and meta descriptions
- Allows the addition of multiple widgets for extra visual functionality

- Can add very valuable plugins for enhancement and extra functionality
- Can provide visitor statistics
- Customisable themes
- To show links to other favourite blogs or websites
- Allows links to other sections in a main website – e.g. a contact us page or further information
- Customisable styles via edit of CSS files
- Users can post from anywhere in the world
- Everything is self-contained – no need for other programs like an HTML editor
- Built in spell checker with live spell checking
- The ability to summaries posts with an automatically generated page which contains the whole post and a link to this page from the main blog.
- The ability to assign multiple tags to any post and be able to display archives by category.
- As the best blogging systems are free open source (e.g. Word Press) there should be no software purchasing costs, running costs, upgrade costs or license fee.

5. KEY FEATURES OF A BLOG FOR VISITORS

- Easy for visitors to navigate and find things of interest to them
- Allows comments on individual posts by visitors (user interactivity)
- Has a spam blocking system
- Shows recent posts in the sidebar
- Previous posts easy to find in the sidebar
- Posts print out just how they look on screen
- Has an RSS feed so visitors are encouraged to subscribe to all posts via email or newsfeed system

- The option to receive posts from a variety of different sources with e-mail capability such as mobile phones, PDA's, web-based e-mail etc.
- To show bookmarking icon so visitors are encouraged to save the site in their favourites
- To facilitate bookmarking facility so visitors can recommend posts to sites like Facebook, Twitter, Delicious, Stumpleupon, Digg, etc therefore helping with bringing new visitors
- To provide sharing facility so visitors can forward posts by email to a friend
- To provide tag cloud so visitors can see the most popular topics
- To provide word search facility
- To provide categories for easy filtered searching by visitors
- To provide archived posts listed by months in the sidebar

6. TYPES OF BLOGGER

Blogs can be personal or professional. They may be private with use internally in an organization or they may be publicly available – this is controlled by the settings on blog site.Blogs can be individual, group or subject blogs. An individual blog is a personal blog reflecting the thoughts of one person. A group blog is a collective effort written by a team or organisation, and a subject blog is written by any number of people, and is focused on a particular topic. Once we have decided on the blog's purpose think about which of these different approaches will work best for us. we may also like to think about developing a set of blog policies to help outline the blog's scope, and focus your target audience.

A. The Niche Expert : These bloggers create niche sites on anything that might have a good prospect of making money – something to do with gadgets or celebrities or credit cards, for instance. They run lots of ads, or put in plenty of affiliate links, or both. These bloggers may well have The 4-Hour Workweek on their shelves.Often, these bloggers are highly motivated and driven. Their content is sometimes of variable quality, but the best niche experts provide real value for readers.

B. The Business Owner : This blogger is part of a fast-growing movement. She produces high-quality content to support her business (which could be anything from running a country pub to an SEO agency). Her posts may cover a range of topics, but all will relate to her business.These bloggers often provide some of the best content on the web. They've got a reputation to maintain, and they set themselves high standards.

C. The Professional Blogger : The Professional Blogger is at a cross between 1 and 2. They see their blogs as integral to their business. They're proud of what they've built, and they write about a topic they love. Unlike the Niche Expert, they're unlikely to have multiple blogs. They use their blogs to make money through a variety of means: membership sites, consulting, ebooks, e-courses, and / or other digital products. They don't tend to have an offline presence (like a store or office) that can visit, unlike the Business Owner. Their content is excellent – it has to be, as it's the cornerstone of their business.

D. The Journal Writer : These bloggers have an 'old-school' blog – one that's similar to a personal journal, often covering a wide range of topics, often in a narrative format. They probably participate in memes, and may have a small or large readership. Some blog irregularly, sometimes posting daily, while at other times not having any fresh posts for months; others stick to a regular schedule. They're usually not concerned about 'monetization' or 'SEO'. They might run a few ads or pop in some affiliate links to help pay their hosting costs – but their blog is primarily a hobby and a place to have fun. They see readers as potential new friends, not potential customers.

E. The Platform-Builder : These bloggers are looking to make a name for themselves, with money a more distant objective. They might be authors current or prospective building a readership for their books, or individuals working in new media who want to impress employers. Platform-builders, like business owners, have a strong incentive to produce great content. They will usually stick fairly closely to one topic. The blogger generally find ads on their blog, and some will avoid affiliate links.

F. The Product Promoter : These bloggers have something to sell: often a book. They can find anywhere buttheir own blog – and some won't have an online home base at all. Instead, they're on a blog tour around the web, with guest posts and interviews on different sites. Product promoters may not see themselves as bloggers at all, especially if they don't have their own blog. They'll often have great insights to share, though some may be unfamiliar with how best to write for the web – host blogs can often help by doing a bit of extra formatting on their guest posts.

G. The Freelancer : These bloggers get paid to write posts for major sites. They may specialize in a particular topic (gardening, healthy eating, personal development) or they may take whatever comes along! Most will write regularly for the same site, often on a weekly or monthly basis. Their content is usually top-notch – after all, they're being paid for it! Their employer will often do some editing to ensure a polished final piece. These bloggers may or may not have their own blog

7. APPLICATIONS OF BLOGS IN LIBRARIES

The following provides a few ideas for blogging in your library. This is just a small selection – blogs are very versatile and there are many more practical applications.

News Gathering and Dissemination : Blogs provide a useful way for librarians to disseminate small snippets of information to their library users. A subject librarian in an academic library might find it useful to gather database updates, new site and service notices and event information in the one place on a blog.

From the Librarian's Desk : Blogging about daily work gives library users an insight into library staff roles and responsibilities. It helps to provide openness and transparency, whilst informing of library news and events.

Community Building : As librarians we are part of a group of professionals that benefit from the sharing of good practice and experiences. Blogs can be a very timely way to offer advice and commentary on current library issues.

Library Resources : Raise the profile of the resources in library by blogging about their features. If we have a collection of resources for speakers of other languages, why not invite a few people using these materials to blog about them, and build an online community.

Special projects : Are we building a new library, refurbishing a new section, or other library developments that are visible to your library community? Blogging about the project will allow our users to engage in the project and become involved in decision making, and photos or videos of progress can add interest to our blog.

Task Groups : Use a blog to capture and collect the thoughts of members involved in a task group. Blogs have built in archive features to record our work and tagging can be used to categorise sections.

Reflective Journaling : Blogs don't have to be public affairs. Think about our own professional development and chronicle our activities on a blog. It's amazing how a few minutes spent reflecting on our daily activities adds up so we can see a path of progression and achievements. If appropriate, share these thoughts with our colleagues so they also have a record of our activities.

8. MERITS OF BLOGS

The merits of blogs from an organizational perspective include the following:

1. The consumer and citizen are potentially better informed and this can only be good for the long-term health of our societies and economies.
2. Blogs have potential to help the organization develop stronger relationships and brand loyalty with its customers, as they interact with the 'human face' of the organization through blogs.
3. Blogs, in an intranet environment, can be an excellent way of sharing knowledge within the organization.
4. Blogs can be a positive way of getting feedback, and keeping our finger on the pulse, as readers react to certain pieces, suggest story ideas, etc.
5. Blogs can build the profile of the writer, showcasing the organization as having talent and expertise.

9. DEMERITS OF BLOGS

The demerits of blogs are:

1. Most people don't have very much to say that's interesting, and/or are unable to write down their ideas in a compelling and clear manner.
2. Some people who have most time to write have least to say, and the people who have most to say don't have enough time to write it. Thus, the real expertise within the organization lays hidden.
3. Blogs are easy to start and hard to maintain. Writing coherently is one of the most difficult and time-consuming tasks for a human being to undertake. So, far from blogs being a cheap strategy, they are

a very expensive one, in that they eat up time. As a result, many blogs are not updated, thus damaging rather than enhancing the reputation of the organization.

4. Organizations are not democracies. The Web makes many organizations look like disorganizations, with multiple tones and opinions. Contrary to what some might think, the average customer prefers it if the organization they are about to purchase from is at least somewhat coherent.

10. LIBRARIES BLOGS

1. *LISLog*
2. *Library Next*
3. *LISNews.com*
4. *Radio Frequency Identification (RFID)*
5. *Greenstone Blog*
6. *International and Comparative Librarianship*
7. *LISMysore*
8. *Indexing Blog*
9. *LibInfoSpace*
10. *Kendriya Vidyalaya Librarians*

11. BLOGGING SOFTWARE AND PLATFORMS

1. WordPress
2. Blogger
3. Twitter
4. Tumblr
5. Posterous
6. Squarespace
7. TypePad
8. Movable Type
9. Drupal

10. ExpressionEngine
11. Open Diary
12. Live Journal
13. Xanga
14. Dead Journal
15. Facebook

12. CONCLUSION

We can conclude that a blog on the internet gives us the opportunity to respond and/or give criticism to the blogger point of view. Blogging has changed the info-hierarchy that we knew. The common man has got more to say today, and his opinions are being heard more often. Before blogging the editors of the large Medias decided what we needed to know, but blogging has changed all of aspects. In the field of Library & Information Science blogs are plying very important role in the point of view of the staff and user. Users demands are fulfilling through library blogs with interaction between the staff and users.

REFERENCES

- Arjun, Dasgupta. 2008 "Blog in Library and Information Services". *IASLIC Bulletin*. Vol.53,no. 4.pp. 241-246
- Blogger, Available at: *http://www.blogger.com*
- Fichter, Darlene, 2003. "Why and How to Use Blogs to Promote Your Library's Services". *Marketing Library Services*.vol.17, no.6.pp 1-4
- G Singh and Shahid,2006. S.M. "Blogs as tools for online information sharing". *Library Philosophy and Practice*. vol.9,no. 1. Available at: *http://unllib.unl.edu/LPP/singh-shahid.html*.
- Natarajan, M,2009. "Blogs: A powerful tool for accessing information". *DESIDOC Bulletin of Information Technology*. vol. 27,no.3
- ODLIS. Blog. Available at http://lu.com/odlis/odlis_w.cfm (Accessed on 24/05/ 2014).
- Prasad, M.R.M,2004. "Weblogs to exploit library and

information services". 2nd International CALIBER11-13th Feb., New Delhi. Pp.566-573.

- Weblog. Wikipedia. Available at: *www.en.wikipedia.org./ wiki/weblog.*
- Whitney, Davinson Turley,2008. "Blogs and RSS: powerful Information Management Tools." *Library Hi Tech News*.vol.22,no.10. pp.28-29.
- Young, M.L,2007. "Blogging: An introductory look at an old pastime in a new medium". *Library High Tech News*. vol.8. pp.27-28.

9

Benefits of Institutional Repositories in the Society

Amandeep Kaur
Assistant Librarian, DAV University, Jalandhar (Punjab)

ABSTRACT

An institutional repository is the collective intellectual output of an institution recorded in a form that can be preserved and exploited. This article briefly outlines the need for repositories such as Dspace, their role, benefits and drawbacks. It concludes that repositories are the key to the ability of institutions to respond to future needs for more dynamic cross-boundary communications services.

Key words : Institutional repositories, IR Software, Digital Library Initiatives in india

INTRODUCTION

Institutional repositories are designed to manage, host, preserve and enable distribution of the scholarly output of an institution. Institutional repositories are "a managed storage system with content deposited on a personal, departmental, institutional, national, regional, or consortia basis, providing services to designated communities, with content drawn from the range of digital resources that support learning, teaching and research".

DEFINITION

There are a number of definitions for Institutional Repositories "IR". Out of many two definitions (lynch, 2003); (ware, 2004) are given as under:

On Institutional Repositories Clifford Lynch states that "In my view, a university based institutional repository is a set of services that a university offers to the members of its community for the management and dissemination of digital material created by the institution and its community members. It is most essentially an organizational commitment to the stewardship of these digital materials, including long – term preservation where appropriate, as well as organization and access or distribution".

According to Mark ware " An Institutional Repository is defined to be a web – based database (repository) of scholarly material which is institutionally defined(as opposed to a subject based repository) cumulative and perpetual(a collection of record); open and interoperable (e.g.: using OAI – Compliant software); and thus collects, stores and disseminates (is part of the process of scholarly communication). In addition, most would include long-term preservation of digital materials as a key function of IRs".

SELECTED OPEN SOURCE SOFTWARE FOR CREATING IRS

The most important factor in development of an OAI compliant institutional repositories is open source software, which are available for the development of an institutional repositories in university/institutional libraries. Some important open source software is given below.

DSpace : http://cdsware.cem.cem/www.dspace.org

EPrints : http://cdsware.cem.ch/www.eprints.org

I – Tor : http://cdsware.cem.ch/www.i-tor.org/en

MyCoRe : http://cdsware.cem.ch/www.mycore.de/eng/index.html

CDSWare : http://cdsware.cem.ch/

FEDORA : http://www.fedora.info/

DIGITAL LIBRARY INITIATIVES IN INDIA

1. Library Consortium in India :
   a. CSIR E-Journal Consortium : *http://rdpp.csir.res.in/csir_acsir/Home.aspx*
   b. UGC-Infonet Consortium : *http://www.inflibnet.ac.in/econ/*
2. Scholarly science journals:-
   a. Proceedings of the Indian academy of science : *http://www.ias.ac.in/*
   b. Indian National Science Academy : *http://www.insa.ac.in/*
3. Theses and dissertation:-
   a. IIT Bombay : *http://www.library.iitb.ac.in/*
   b. Vidya nidhi : *http://www.vidyanidhi.org.in/*
4. Institutional repositories:-
   a. Indian Institute of Technology, Delhi : *www.eprint.iitd.ac.in/*
   b. Indian Institute of science, Bangalore : *http://eprints.iisc.ernet.in/*
5. E-Books:-
   a. Universal Digital Library Project : *http://www.dli.gov.in/*
   b. Digital Library of India : *http://www.new.dli.ernet.in/*
6. Manuscripts:-
   a. National mission for manuscripts : *http://namami.nic.in/*
   b. Archives of Indian Labour V.V. Giri National Labour Institute : *http://www.indialabourarchives.org/*

7. Newspaper:
   a. Times of India (epaper): *http://epaper.timesofindia.com/index.asp*
   b. Dinamalar (epaper) : *http://epaper.dinamalar.com/*
8. Online Courseware:
   a. National Programme on Technology Enhanced Learning (NPTEL) (*http://www.nptel.iitm.ernet.in/*)
9. Open access at metadata level:-
   a. Inflibnet : *http://web.inflibnet.ac.in/*
10. Other major initiatives:
   a. Traditional Knowledge Digital Library (TKDL) : *http://203.200.90.71/IndiaTkdl/index.asp*
   b. National Library, Kolkata : *(www.nlindia.org)*

OBJECTIVES OF IR

The four main objectives for having an institutional repositories are:

1. To provide open access to institutional research output by self-archiving it;
2. To create global visibility for an institution's scholarly research;
3. To collect content in a single location;
4. To store and preserve other institutional digital assests, including unpublished or otherwise easily lost literature such as theses or technical reports.
5. Manages and measures research and teaching activities.
6. Enables and encourages interdisciplinary approaches to research.
7. Facilitates the development and sharing of digital teaching material and aids.

MAJOR STEPS FOR DEVELOPING IR

There are many steps involved while planning for establishing the IRs in any university/institutional libraries. All these steps must be considered to make this initiative success. These steps are as follows

- Digital preservation policy
- Selection of documents for IRs/ conversion in digital format
- Archiving policy
- Taking policy decisions to establish institutional repositories / Knowledge bank.
- Self – archiving of documents
- Providing library and information services to end users;
- Open access initiatives.

USEFULNESS OF IRS / KB

- Cost savings
- Avoid Duplication of efforts
- Broaden communication process
- Wide user audience
- Reduction in time in announcing the findings
- IRs has no limit for publication of articles unlike to traditional printed or online journal where page limit.

BENEFITS FOR MAKING THE INSTITUTIONAL REPOSITORIES OPEN ACCESS

- Opening up outputs of the institution to a worldwide audience to enthral the attention of needy scholars;
- Maximizing the visibility and impact of these outputs as a result, hence the user will rely on the portal for future reference;
- Showcasing the institution to interested

constituencies – prospective staff, prospective students and other stakeholders,

- Collecting and curating digital outputs;
- Managing and measuring research and teaching activities;
- Providing a workspace for work –in-progress, and for collaborative or large-scale projects;
- Enabling and encouraging interdisciplinary approaches to research;
- Facilitating the development and sharing of digital teaching materials and aids, and
- Supporting student endeavours, providing access to theses and dissertations and a location for the development of e-portfolios.

ADVANTAGES OF INSTITUTIONAL REPOSITORIES

Some of these benefits will have been key drivers for the development of a repository whilst others may be unanticipated. Different repository models (research only repository, learning and teaching materials repository, mixed content repository, open repository) will have different benefits for each stakeholder group. The following are some of the possible advantages for different groups:

- Maintaining and building on institutional reputations nationally & globally
- Attracting new staff and students to institutions
- Increased transparency and quality of learning materials
- Shares expertise efficiently within institutions
- Supports storage, management, preservation, attribution and retrieval of student content
- Supports the altruistic notion that sharing knowledge is in line with academic traditions

- and a good thing to do Supports preservation of learning resources.
- Facilitates presentation of resources for accreditation bodies
- Enhancing connections with external stakeholders by making resources visible
- Repository content is readily searchable both locally and globally
- Allows an institution to manage their intellectual property by raising awareness of
- copyright issues and facilitating the recording of relevant rights information A repository that contains high quality content could be used as 'shop window' or
- marketing tool to entice staff, students and funding Repositories can store other types of content that isn't necessarily published, sometimes
- known as 'grey literature' A repository may be an important tool in managing an institution's research assessment or
- quality assessment submission Repositories could provide cost savings in the long run provided that a significant amount
- of content is deposited in them Offers greater flexibility over websites with better security and preservation of various
- kinds of digital materials through the collection of standardised metadata about each item

CHALLENGES OF INSTITUTIONAL REPOSITORIES

The communication among the scientific world is poor due to low bandwidth and poor information infrastructure in developing countries to generate adequate amount of digital resources or e-resources are very important problems, which causes hindrances developing institutional repositories. Quality control of digital resources generated and archives in IRs is also one of the important problems which must be addressed properly.

CONCLUSION

Institutional repositories play a very important role in scholarly communication and there are many sources of information within the research arena where the user can search for information. The development of institutional repositories is still in its fancy but a number of important lessons have already emerged. In addition to supporting more traditional scholarship, IRs could pay an important role in supporting alternative forms of journal publishing. Open access through institutional repositories is a low – cost and low – barrier strategy for achieving this mission.

REFERENCES

1. Barton.M.R. and Warters, M.M, 2004. Creating an Institutional Repository: LEADIRS Workbook.
2. Chang, S.H., 2003. "Institutional Repositories: the library's new role".*OCLC systems and services*. Vol.19, pp.77-79.
3. Crow, R., 2002. "The Case for institutional Repositories – a SPRAC position paper" *SPARC.*
4. Sharma, P.L, 2007. Institutional Repositories: An Essential tool for information and knowledge sharing, Faridabad.

10
Library 2.0

Anamika
Librarian, S D College, Barnala

ABSTRACT

Social media has pervaded all spheres of life ranging from the personal to the political. It is revolutionising the whole world in a variety of ways. No business, professional or personal activity is today imaginable without social media. As it also spreads its reach in the academy, it is becoming a vital appendage to the libraries. After initial reluctance to include it in services and larger outreach, today the library community has harnessed social media in various ways for better and quicker services. The immediate and wide connect it offers has led to a paradigm shift in the field of library and information sciences. However, as it is a developing scenario, it will still take more time and many more adjustments to become a fully integral part of the library system.

HOW WEB 2.0 CHANGED THE WORLD

Computer-technology thinker and activist Tim O'Reilly popularised the term Web 2.0 nearly a decade ago. Those were the times when the dot-com bubble had burst in the United States and a large number of computer companies had collapsed. People had started thinking that the internet was an overhyped fad. Web 2.0 meant the next stage of the technological phenomenon of the World Wide Web which was the basis of the internet. The concept of Web 2.0 was based on the idea that the dot-com burst was just a stage in the technological progress and what lay ahead was even more exciting and revolutionary: the interactive internet rather than the static information storehouse that it mostly had been. One early mark of the transition from Web 1.0 to Web 2.0 was replacement of Encyclopedia Britannica and similar resources such as Encarta with the interactive and collective enterprise called Wikipedia. After that came the revolutionary blogs that changed the way the world expressed itself, followed by Facebook and Twitter. Today, the world in all its dimensions, (personal, public and professional) cannot be imagined without the interactive World Wide Web.

THE RISE OF THE SOCIAL MEDIA

The Web 2.0 heralded an unprecedented phenomenon of social networking through engaging websites such as Wikipedia, Facebook, Flickr and Twitter. The new concepts of syndication, weblink and online groups offered a variety of interactive experience to the browsers. If Wen 1,0 was all about information storage, Web 2.0 was aboit information sharing. Typically, a social media website allows you to post your profile, upload your information, get exposed to similar profiles and information and share your information and connect with others in many innovative ways such as 'likes' on Facebook or retweets on Twitter. On a blog, you can not only upload information ut also link to similar blogs, get other bloggers to subscribe to your information feed and comment on other blogs and get comments on your own.

The huge popularity of these web-based innovations led to the term social media, for they had brought together the society like nothing else in the past. Twitter has 284 million monthly active users and 500 million Tweets are sent per day while Facebook has 1.35 billion monthly active users, according to the company websites. Very soon more than half of the world will be active online. This coming together of people has had far-reaching consequences. Twitter and Facebook have even helped mobilise mass movements such as the Arab Spring and the Anna Hazare's movement against corruption. Social media has started influencing voting patterns too. It has become the main platform for not only marketing but buying and selling too.

THE LIBRARY 2.0

The transition from Web 1.0 to Web 2.0 was basically a shift for a static model of information exchange to a dynamic one. Since the academy too is about about the exchange of knowledge and information, it was natural for thee changes in the web to start reflecting in the academic systems of information exchange, i.e. libraries. The two could not remain mutually exclusive. Social media was originally a personal information-sharing platform but soon it became a means to share all kinds of information. In no time, teachers and students began using it enthusiastically. While many in the field of library and information regarded Web 2.0 as another passing fad, slowly there were people who also saw it threatening, especially when Google began scanning library books and putting them online. Today, social media has come to be an essential part of all kinds of activity in the world and libraries too are finding it a welcome addition.

It is not that libraries were untouched by Web 1.0. We saw many libraries putting up online catalogues. So it is quite natural today for libraries to take to the dynamic tools of Web 2.0. Though the idea of Library 2.0 means several things to different people, its defining feature is diverse interaction between users and library, among users, between users and librarians and among librarians. It is a user-centric model and has innovative ways of bringing the user closer to the library with the help of blogs, social networking websites and multimedia resources.

One of the most comprehensive pictures of Library 2.0 and its components is the model of Library 2.0 presented by Holmberg, Huvila, Kronqvist-Berg, and Widén-Wulff (Holmberg, K., Huvila, I., Kronqvist-Berg, M., & Widén-Wulff, G. 2009). This model of Library 2.0 consists of seven building blocks: interactivity, participation, users, social aspects, technology, Web 2.0, and libraries.

A whitepaper on the use of social media by libraries (Taylor & Francis 2014) says the early experiments with Facebook and MySpace were beginning to show promise by 2008. An article (Chu M and Nalani-Meulemans Y 2008) which showed that librarians displaying their online status as 'on' or 'off' helped users identify and connect with them. In another article from 2007 (Charnigo L and Barnett-Ellis P 2007), the Kimbel Library in the Coastal Carolina University was highlighted as providing a range of services through Facebook, such as library tours and promotion of resources. "An additional and unexpected benefit was that these activities also helped forge closer working relationships between staff, simply by virtue of getting to know each other on a more personal level through their social media accounts." The whitepaper cites several studies on the widespread use of social media in libraries in recent times. A 2012 study (Kai-Wah Chu, S. & Du, H. S. 2012) shows how use of social media by the library has now become mainstream. In this survey of libraries in Asia, North America and Europe, 71 per cent were found to be using social media tools with a further 13 per cent saying they planned to use them. Facebook and Twitter were the most commonly used tools.

The survey conducted for the whitepaper in 2014 with the international library community too reflected the trends. It received 497 responses in which over 70 per cent of librarians felt that the use of social media was important. This research comprised three focus groups (one held with UK-based librarians, one with librarians based in India, and one with US-based librarians); 10 individual in-depth phone interviews; a Twitter party; on online survey (distributed in July 2014 with 497 responses); and desk research to identify relevant studies and commentary articles.

The white paper states, "From our survey, over 70% of libraries are using social media tools, and 60% have had a social media account for three years or longer. 30% of librarians are posting at least daily. Facebook and Twitter remain the most popular channels currently, but the range of channels being used is expanding rapidly; there is a particular acceleration of interest in visual channels such as YouTube, Pinterest and Snapchat. Specialist research networking sites such as ResearchGate and Academia.edu are seen as having potential, but their perceived disconnect with publishers and the library community is a barrier. "

THE PARADIGM SHIFT IN LIBRARIES

A 2011 article in Information Today (Kho, N. D. 2011) lists many ways in which libraries are benefiting from the use of social media. It quotes Keri Thompson, head of the web services department at the Smithsonian Institution Libraries, who has seen the communication and marketing benefits of the organisation's social media efforts firsthand. Thompson mentions recent efforts by the Biodiversity Heritage Library at the Smithsonian as an example. BHL is a consortium of 12 natural history and botanical libraries that cooperate to digitize and to make accessible the legacy literature of biodiversity that is held in their collections. "Once they took over the @bhl account on Twitter," says Thompson, "We saw a 10-fold increase in followers within two weeks."

Social media is impacting libraries in several profound ways. It turns the library into a virtual space so that anyone, anywhere can have access to the basic features. The most primary use of social media for libraries is to put out information in the public domain. It helps them inform the reader not only about new services or additions but also about several events. Promotion of library resources becomes very easy with the use of social media. Client servicing can be prompt as users can be accessed quickly on Twitter and Facebook. Social media is not only helping foster user communities but also forges relations between libraries and among the library professional. The areas where the use of social media is making a concrete impact are promotion of content and customer service in real time. It is expected to also enhance teaching and learning and institutional capacity building in the whole sphere of library and information sciences.

ADVANTAGES AND CHALLENGES

The main advantage of social media for libraries is that it costs little but is prompter tha nay other means. A mere presence on the internet can lead to a huge enhancement in the services of a library. Since it is so pervasive in the society today, it also does not require the library staff to get any special training to use it. If client servicing is quick with social media, so is the user feedback. It can also offer an effective model for inhouse interaction for the library staff and foster a sense of community and purpose among them. Since personal and public are interlinked online, the use of social media helps build a more personal interaction between users and the staff which leads to a better knowledge of user preferences.

However, it is not without its own challenges. Though operation of popular websites requires no specialised knowledge, new applications designed exclusively for the library may require special technological knowledge. Increasing and maintaining internet presence can be quite time-consuming. Social media is largely an informal space where delivering formal services can require library staff to maintain the thin line between being totally casual and more accessible.

Today, social media is also a highly contested space rife with several controversies. Time to time, it requires government oversight. Until social media is fully integrated into real systems of governance, its use will be fraught with risks and it can at best act as supplement to the offline library services. However, there is no denying the fact that in future, social media is going to redefine the libraries as we know them today. The survey conducted for the Taylor & Francis white paper (Taylor & Francis 2014) found that 88 per cent of the respondents felt that social media would become even more important to the libraries in the future.

REFERENCES

- Charnigo L and Barnett-Ellis P., 2007. 'Checking out Facebook.com: The impact of a digital trend on academic libraries'. *Information Technology and Libraries.* Vol. 26, no. 1. pp. 23–34
- Chu M and Nalani-Meulemans Y., 2008. 'The problems and potential of MySpace and Facebook usage in academic libraries'. *Internet Reference Services Quarterly.* Vol.13,no.1. pp. 69–85
- Holmberg, K., Huvila, I., Kronqvist-Berg, M., and Widén-Wulff, G., 2009. 'What is Library 2.0?'. *Journal of Documentation,* vol.65.no.4. pp. 668-681
- Kai-Wah Chu, S. & Du, H. S. 2012, 'Social Networking Tools for Academic Libraries'. *Journal of Librarianship and Information Science,* vol.45,no.1. pp. 64-75
- Kho, N. D. 2011, 'Social media in libraries: Keys to deeper engagement' Information Today, vol.28. no.6
- Taylor & Francis, 2014. 'Use of social media by the iibrary: Current practices and future opportunities' Available at: *http://www.tandf.co.uk/journals/access/white-paper-social-media.pdf*

11

Impact of Social Media in Marketing of Library Product and Services

Shaveta

Librarian Amardeep Singh Shergill Memorial College (A University College) Mukandpur Distt. SBS Nagar Punjab

ABSTRACT

The Paper Deals with concept of marketing and its role in library. It highlights activities and medium for promoting library products and services. It discusses how technology is useful in promoting library products and services.

1. INTRODUCTION

In the recent years libraries have taken initiative to introduce IT based products and services. With the help of Information Technology library products can access easily at low cost and in less time. Social Media, Emails , website, LISlinks, e-resources etc. are helpful in promoting library services and products.

2. CONCEPT OF MARKETING

Marketing is a process of caring goods from producers to ultimate consumers. its is a planned process of identifying users' requirement and then producing goods according to target customers and to achieve the goal of organization .

In case of library, marketing means to study information needs of the client, creating consolidated products and then planning ways of informing library clients about these products and services.

3. NEED AND PURPOSE OF MARKETING IN LIBRARY

Libraries Invest huge amount of money on the collection development of library resources. When these resources are remained unutilized resulting wastage of money, time, energy and space. By applying Marketing Principles libraries can come out from this problem of unutilization . Madhusudan (2008) states Information marketing by libraries in India is essential in order to:

- Promote the use of information resources
- Create perception of need and thereby create demand
- Ensure optimum use of information
- Tackle the problem of rising costs of reading material
- Cope with the infonnation explosion
- Improve the image and status of libraries and library Professionals.
- Raise awareness of the range of Library Services, Projects and events and to encourage wider take-up.
- Promote the library's online offer – the website, online renewals.
- Encourage new members to join the library and lapsed members to return

4. PRODUCTS OF LIBRARIES

- Books
- Periodicals
- References Sources

- Manuscripts, Rare Books, Paintings and coins etc.
- Newspapers
- Thesis and Dissertations
- Journals and Magazines
- Bibliographies
- Directories
- Library Pamphlet
- News Bulletin
- Etc.

5. SERVICES OF LIBRARIES

- Reference Services
- Bibliographic Services
- Current Awareness Services
- SDI Services
- Inter Library Loan Services
- Photocopy Services
- OPAC
- Indexing/ Abstracting Services
- Consortia
- Etc

6. SOCIAL MEDIA

Social Media provides several opportunities to reach and interact with the community at wider range.

Social media play a wonderful role in marketing of library product and services. Dr. Ranganathan 's concept of the Five Law of Library Science had the marketing concept at their core . Today the technology is also play a vital role in exploring the concept of the Dr. Ranganathan's Five Law of Library Science :

- First Law; "Books are for use" (Maximize the use of books)

- Second Law, "Every Reader his/her book" (Reader is the prime factor and his /her need must be satisfied)
- Third Law , "Every book its reader" (Find a reader for every Book)
- Fourth Law, "Save the time of reader" (Organize the information in such a way that the reader can access easily)
- Fifth Law, "A library is a growing organism (emphasis is on comprehensive and evolutionary growth)

With the help of social media we can provide right information to right user at right time .

7. TRADITIONAL VS SOCIAL MEDIA MARKETING

Traditional Marketing	*Social Media Marketing*
Time Consuming	Time saving
Expensive cost	effective
Limitation to reach the community	Reachable to the community instantly
Static	Creative
Allows little or no interaction with user community	Brings librarians closer to users and vice versa
One	way Collaborative
Passive	Interactive
Time	bound No time limitation
Limited means for marketing A range of Social Media channels for marketing	Limited means for marketing A range of Social Media channels for marketing

It shows that how the social media has changed the traditional way of marketing from walls of library to the world-wide.

8. TOOLS OF SOCIAL MEDIA

- Twitter
- Facebook
- Blogs
- Instant Messaging
- You Tube
- Flickr
- Ning
- Myspace
- Wikis
- LISlink
- Videoconferencing
- Emails
- Weread , etc.

9. ROLE OF SOCIAL MEDIA IN PROMOTING LIBRARY SERVICES

- Maximize the use of Library
- Capture potential users of the library
- Grab the new users for library
- Make friendly relation between user and library
- Helps to feed user with information
- Helps to make Cooperation with other libraries
- Easy way of Knowledge sharing
- Promote e-learning
- Explore Information resources geographically
- 24×7 availability of information
- Modernize the library image and e-reputation
- Spread news and services alerts

10. PROBLEMS IN USING SOCIAL MEDIA IN LIBRARY

- Lack of Knowledge

- Lack of Trained Staff
- Lack of Funds
- Lack of adequate Infrastructure
- Electricity Problem
- Slow speed of Internet
- Inadequate training opportunities for staff
- Psychological not prepare.
- Unaware users

CONCLUSION

To conclude, Marketing of Library Product is essential for libraries to satisfy the information need of library users. With the help of technology Libraries can actively play their role. Government, Organizations, UGC and institutions must provide training to staff. Seminars and conferences are also useful in providing professional skill and knowledge to latest tool of marketing.

REFERENCES

Chopra,H.S., 1996. Marketing of information services and Indian scenario.Jaipur:Rawat Publicatiobns

Kumar, P.S.G., 1998. Fundamental of information science. New Delhi: S.Chand

Stanton,W.J., 1981. Fundamentals of marketing . New York: McGraw-Hill

http://crl.du.ac.in/ical09/papers/index_files/ical-79_73_172_2_RV.pdf

http://culturehive.co.uk/resources/using-social-media-to-market-library-services

http://docs.lib.purdue.edu/cgi/viewcontent.cgi?article=1111&context=iatul

http://www.idpublications.org/wp-content/uploads/2014/07/APPLICATION.pdf

http://oedb.org/ilibrarian/10-social-media-marketing-tips-for-libraries/

http://www.webology.org/2012/v9n1/a93.html

12

Digital Library Services With Social Networking

Ashu Tyagi
Librarian,
Plato Public School, Delhi -110092

ABSTRACT

Digital library is defined as the collection of services and the collection of information objects and their organization, structure and presentation that support users in dealing with information objects available directly or indirectly via electronic / digital means.The concept of digital libraries in India began in the mid 1990s with the spread of information technology, the internet and the support of the Central Government. In 1996, this concept was recognized during the Conference on Digital Libraries organized by the Society of Information Science at Bangalore. Though a few libraries have made attempts earlier in this direction, the digital library initiative in India is still at budding stage.Today there are umpteen numbers of Digital Libraries worldwide; some of the important Digital Libraries in India have been highlighted here .Hence, this paper highlights the feature, digital library software,digital library initiatives and their issues in India.

Keywords : Digital library, Digital library software, Digital library initiatives, India.

INTRODUCTION

Digital library refers to a collection that constitutes

electronic resources, accessible through the World Wide Web. It often contains electronic versions of books, photographs, videos that are owned by a "physical" library.

Digital Libraries are electronic libraries in which large number of geographically distributed users can access the contents of large and diverse repositories of e-objects. E- objects include networked text, images, maps, sounds, and videos, catalogues of merchandise and scientific business and Government datasets. They also include hypertext, hypermedia and multimedia compositions. The important characteristics of Digital Libraries are the storage of information in digital form, direct usage of communication networks for accessing and obtaining information and copying by either downloading or online/offline printing from a master file.

Information and Communication Technologies (ICTs) have brought significant changes in all- round development of the society through transmission of information. Application of information technology to Library and Information Science has provided wider opportunities in archiving and accessing knowledge in the digitized form besides conservation and preservation of the traditional knowledge. Digitization of materials will provide enhanced access to the electronic information sources and the users can access the digital content irrespective of time and space boundaries. In India, digital library initiatives were undertaken initially with a view to preserve the art, culture and heritage of the country. Some special libraries are also engaged in digital library initiatives in a limited way.

DEFINITION

Digital Library Foundation (DLF) has defined on digital libraries as: "Digital libraries are organizations that provide the resources, including the specialized staff, to select, structure, offer intellectual access to, interpret, distribute, preserve the integrity of, and ensure the persistence over time of collections of digital works so that they are readily and economically available for use by a defined community or set of communities."

Digital libraries provide resources, including specialized staff to choose, that is the plan, structure, they are easily and economically, so that the intellectual access to interpret, distribute, preserve the integrity of digital works, storage time and continue to ensure the targeted community or communities, is available for use by groups. The term 'digital library' of the organization, intellectual accessibility, or service in the nation may refer to a collection of symptoms without a reference. We listen to the digital library as the World Wide Web seems to be a game that has a specific meaning. But the words are stored in the computer-based system for the collection of more specific and refer to the organization, or can. The digital libraries and on the scope for the development of functional requirements serve as the default view on the DLF. Digital libraries, especially in jobs and resources, especially staff with a variety of intellectual resources in the organization, but on the model of traditional libraries, or even within the context of traditional libraries do not need to. Digital libraries within traditional libraries needed by the resources, they are kind of different. For example, for storage and retrieval, digital libraries, almost completely, computer and electronic - depends on network systems, and the necessary staff, equipment and system engineering skills, instead of traditional catalogers and Reference Librarians' skills, ranks high, "outsourcing" the work of the library collection and experiment with distributed repositories.

There is no single definition for Digital Libraries. The definition evolves as research progresses and we learn more about digital libraries. Some of the current definitions are:

- Digital libraries are systems that combine the

machinery of digital computing, storage and communication, the content, and software needed to reproduce, emulate, and extend the services of collecting, cataloging, finding and disseminating information offered by traditional libraries based on paper and other materials. A full service digital library must not only fulfill all essential services provided by traditional libraries but also make good use of the advantages of digital technology.

- Digital libraries are viewed as systems providing a community of users with coherent access to a large, organized repository of information and knowledge. This organization of information is characterized by the absence of prior detailed knowledge of the uses of the information. The ability of the user to access, reorganize, and utilize this repository is enriched by the capabilities of digital technologies .
- The concept of a "digital library" is not merely equivalent to a digitized collection with information management tools. It is rather an environment to bring together collections, services, and people in support of the full life cycle of creation, dissemination, use, and preservation of data, information, and knowledge.

FEATURES

Digital libraries have attracted almost all the developed and developing countries due to its features and the opportunities it extend to the information providers and information seekers. The digital library has the information in the electronic form and electronic media facilitates the access to information available in digital form at different places. It offers new levels of access to broader audiences of users and new opportunities for library and information science field to advance both theory and practice. They contain information collections predominantly in digital or electronic form.

The term digital library on every conceivable subject, different types of information technology implies different things to many different people. Many different types of information available on any conceivable topic library Internet appears to serve several functions. Arms of information stored in digital format and are accessible on the network along with associated services, managed data storage means defines a digital library. Some people are just a new way of carrying a library of functions. In the digital library, reader e-journals, databases, online magazine, and will have access to e-books. Similarly, rare books and manuscripts will be available in digital form. Thus, all of the traditional library resources in digital library will be accessible in electronic form. The role of the librarian in the digital library will be the same but in different ways. Total free online books and free online journal data will be collected.

Digital library research related work in the long history of information retrieval, database, and user interface, networks, data profiles, classification and organization is built on, library automation, publishing and other areas of the digital library user interfaces networks, data networking, etc. You will need a modern librarian will be responsible for dissemination of information than a conventional one. Internet is the most important component of the data. Information from the Internet to access information online, as well as traditional physical libraries can draw. The data repository of documents is indexed for efficient search, where an organized collection. Digital library users as a repository to see that this is a group of distributed repositories.

Access the list of users online on the Internet for a new acquisition and make them available to local libraries are available. New cataloging standardization of tools and knowledge to new domains and formats. Another important issue is indexed. Roles of digital libraries through global Internet information resources available to them to make a large array is defined as. Bibliography Index to the creation of a large amount of content, accuracy and completeness of Retrievals subsequent increases, which adds more value to the service.

DIGITAL LIBRARY SOFTWARE

There are many digital library softwares available, proprietary as well as open source, and most of them conform to international standards. Some of the popular Open Source Softwares for digital libraries, which are in use internationally, are 'DSpace', 'Dienst', 'Eprints', 'Fedora', 'Greenstone' etc. For want of control and clarity, Greentone, EPrints and DSpace are discussed in this paper

(a) Greenstone Digital Library Software : The Greenstone (http://www.greenstone.org) Digital Library Software (GSDL) is a top of the line and internationally renowned Open Source Software system for developing digital libraries, promoted by the New Zealand Digital Library project research group at the University of Waikato, headed by Dr. Ian H. Witten, and is sponsored by the UNESCO. A typical digital library built with Greenstone will contain many collections, individually organized. Easily maintained, collections can be augmented and rebuilt automatically .

(b) D-space : DSpace (http://www.dspace.org) is a digital repository platform jointly developed by Hewlett-Packard and MIT Libraries collaborating over two years. DSpace provides the basic functionality required to operate an institutional digital repository, and is intended to serve as a base for future development to address long term preservation and access issues. Dspace is very good system for capturing, storing, indexing, preserving and redistributing digital research materials. Universities and Research Institutions worldwide use Dspace as an institutional repository, a learning object repository, for records management, and more. Dspace manages and distributes the digital items and allow creation, indexing and searching of associated metadata to locate and retrieve them.

(c) Eprints : EPrints is free software developed by the "University of Southampton, England". EPrints repository collects preserves and disseminates in digital format the research output created by a research community. It enables the community to deposit their preprints; post prints and other scholarly publications using a web interface, and organizes these publications for easy retrieval. It is the world's first, most widely used, and by far the most functional of all the available OA IR software's.

DIGITAL LIBRARY INITIATIVES IN INDIA

During the past five years, India has seen several Digital Library initiatives at the institutional, organizational and at national levels. Some of them are quite successful while others are making significant progress.

Some of the major initiatives on Digital Libraries in India are furnished below:

a) Digital Library of India : The mission is to create a portal for the Digital Library of India which will foster creativity and free access to all human knowledge. It is piloted by the Office of the Principle Scientific Advisor to the Governmentof India, Ministry of Communication and Information Technology with Indian Institute of Science and Carnegie Mellon University, USA as partners. Eleven academic institutions, six religious and cultural institutions, four government and research agencies, and two research institutions in India are participating in this programme.

b) INFLIBNET (www.dspace.inflibnet.ac.in) : INFLIBNET has developed a digital library by using

Dspace, an open source software. So far INFIBNET has digitised their conference proceeding namely, Caliber and Planner. INFLIBNET provide users the facility to download the full-text articles from its databases..

c) Kalasampada (http://www.ignca.gov. in/dgt_0001.htm) : Recognising the need to encompass and preserve the distributed fragments of Indian art and culture, and to serve as a major resource centre for the arts, the Indira Gandhi National Centre for the Arts (IGNCA) in collaboration with Ministry of Communication and Information Technology, initiated a project, Kalasampda (digital library: resources of Indian cultural heritage), for the development of databank of cultural heritage. Kalasampada provides access to over couple of lakhs of manuscripts, over a lakhs of slides, thousands of rare books, rare photographs, audio, and video along with highly researched publications of the IGNCA from a single window.

d) Librarians Digital Library (https://drtc.isibang.ac.in/) : This library has been developed by Documentation Research & Training Centre (DRTC), and contains full-text of papers/articles related to Indian librarianship. Presently, it contains full-text papers submitted in DRTC seminars,papers submitted by LIS professionals, and theses/dissertations of students. It also has plans to include conference proceedings of Indian LIS Associations.

e) Nalanda Digital Library (http://www.nalanda.nitc.ac.in/) : Nalanda Digital Library initiated in 1999 at the National Institute of Technology (NIT), Calicut, is one of the largest digital libraries in the country. Nalanda helps members of the NIT in meeting their academic and research needs by providing timely and up-to-date information with value added services in all the areas of science, engineering, and technology.

f) National Library of India (*www.nlindia.org*) :

The library preserves the scanning and archives the rare and brittle books and other documents on compact disc. The library will digitise the books and documents published before 1900 and available Indian publications prior to 1920. So far, 6,600 selected books in Indian and English languages have already been scanned and stored.

g) Raman Research Institute (http:// dspace.rri.res.in/) : Raman Research Institute has digitised the research publications of the faculty, students, and the publication of the institute. The Institute has also digitised its annual reports and newspaper clippings.

h) Universal Digital Library (http:// *www.iiita. ac.in/research/udl.html*) : Universal Digital Library seeks to digitise books of common interest to different communities of interest (COI) and make them available in a manner that is independent of language, location, and time. A complete solution for this was developed by Carnegie-Mellon sUniversity, USA involving state-of-the-art planetary scanners for scanning, cropping, OCR, and XML converting. Apart from Indian Institute of Science (IISc), other Indian institutions involved in this project are NCST Mumbai, and IIIT, Hyderabad.

i) Vidyanidhi Digital Library and e-scholarship Portal (http://210.212. 200.226/index.html) : Vidyanidhi is an information infrastructure, a digital library, a portal of resources and tools, and facilities doctoral research in India. Vidyanidhi is envisioned to evolve as a national repository and a consortium for e-theses through participation and partnership with universities, academic institutions, and other stake holders. It will enhance the access to Indian theses and will also enlarge the reach and audience for Indian doctoral research works.

j) Electronic Theses and Dissertations Digital Library : Indian Institute of Technology Bombay has established electronic submission of theses and dissertations (ETD) since 1999-2000, in addition to its printed copy, the Central Library maintains ETD server and help students in online submission at URL.In addition to that Central Library (IITB) digitized abstracts of Ph.D. theses submitted to the institute and made it available on Internet with bibliographic details, using Greenstone Digital Library Software.

k) Archives of Indian Labour : The Archives of Indian Labour was set up in July, 1998 as a collaborative project of V.V. Giri National Labour Institute and the Association of Indian Labour Historians. The core activities of the archive are Digital Archiving, Research, Collection, Public Interface & Dissemination. It was instituted in order to address the urgent need for preservation of rapidly decaying documents and material on labour and to provide for greater public access to the same, as It was felt that documents and data on Indian Labour are being irretrievably lost due to lack of an organized initiative to preserve these documents in the country. The archive, apart from being a repository of documents also builds collections and initiates research in the field of labour history.

l) Indian National digital Library in Engineering Science & Technology : The Ministry of Human Resource Development (MHRD) has set-up the Indian National Digital Library in Engineering Sciences and Technology (INDEST) Consortium on the recommendation made by the Expert Group. INDEST Consortium is the most ambitious initiative taken up so far in the country. It welcomes other institutions to join and offers highly discounted rates of subscription and better terms of agreement with the publishers. INDEST Consortium presently include ACM Digital Library, ASCE Journals, ASMe Journals, Capitaline, Euromonitor (GMID), IEL Online, Indian Standards, Nature, ProQuest Science,

Sciencedirect, Springerlink and bibliographic databases of Compendex, Inspec and MathSciNet.

m) Mobile Digital Library (Dware Dware Gyan Sampada) : For spreading and promoting literacy among the common citizens, Internet enabled Mobile Digital Library was brought to use. Mobile Van with satellite connection for Internet connectivity is used. The van is also fitted with printer, and binding machine for providing bound books to the end user from a single point. This is a product from C-DAC-ERDC Noida.

n) Mukhtabodha Digital Library and Archiving Project : The Mukhtabodha Project is an attempt to create a digital library in Indian languages specially the ancient texts on palm leaves, birch tree barks etc.

o) National Institute of Advanced Studies (NIAS), Bangalore : This institution has started digitization of paintings and the Microfilming of Indian Publication Project (MIPP). The NIAS has also started work on rare manuscript preservation projects for both microfilm and microfiche.

p) Centre for Development of Advanced Computing (C-DAC) Digital Library of Art Masterpieces: This is the first initiative of its kind in Asia and it will digitize 200 rare paintings of Rabindranath Tagore and Amrita Shergill from the National Gallery of Modern Arts (NGMA). The infrastructure to host this digital library will be located at the C-DAC Bangalore. C-DAC and Hewlett Packard launched the joint initiative "When Art Meets Technology" for digital preservation, restoration, and dissemination of art from the NGMA at Bangalore on February 4, 2003.

DIGITAL LIBRARY DEVELOPMENT ISSUES IN INDIA

There are umpteen number of problems the Digital Library development teams face in India while they embark on the digital library development as well as during the progress phase. Some of the prominent and predominant among them include the following :

i. Lack of proper Information & Communication Technology (ICT) Infrastructure Digital Libraries demand cutting edge IT and Communication infrastructure such as:

a) High end and powerful Servers; Structured LAN with Broadband Intranet facilities, ideally optical fibre based Gigabit networks;

b) Required number of Workstations capable of providing online information services, computing and multimedia applications;

c) Internet connectivity with sufficient bandwidth, capable of meeting the informational and computational requirement of the user community;

There are many more related facilities / services which are highly essential in an ideal digital library environment. It is observed that the ICT infrastructure in most of the Institutions / Organizations, barring exceptions, are not up to the desired level so as to run advanced digital library services to the optimum level.

ii. Rigidity in the publishers' policies and data formats : Having successfully installed and configured a digital library does not qualify a library to automatically populate all its digital collection into the digital library. One has to obtain publisher's consent and copyright permissions for the same. Digital library softwares usually accept and process all popular and standard digital formats such as HTML, Word, RTF, PPT, or PDF. Most of the publishers put their materials in their own proprietary e-book reader formats, from which the text extraction becomes almost impossible. A vast majority of the scholarly content rests in journal literature and due to copyright issues they cannot be easily (almost impossible) find its way into the local repositories of the digital library.

iii. Lack of ICT Strategies and Policies : A vast majority of the libraries in India do not have laid down policies on ICT panning and strategies to meet the challenges posed by the technology push, the information overload, as well as the demand pull from the users.

iv. Lack of Technical Skills : The Human Resources available in the libraries need time-to-time professional enrichment inputs and rigorous training on the latest technologies which are playing around in the new information environment. The kind of training programmes being imparted in India at the moment are not able to meet the demand in terms of quantity as well as quality.

v. There is a lack of interest on the part of parent institutions and the absence of action plans or priorities are major hindrances. Moreover there is an acute shortage of competent manpower to take up the task of digitizing local content and creating digital information repositories

vi. Copyright / IPR Issues : Issues of copyright, intellectual property, and fair use concerns are posing unprecedented array of problems to the libraries and librarians are struggling to cope with all these related issues in the new digital information environment.

CONCLUSION

Digital Library is nothing but an organized collection of digitized material accessible from a computer over a network. Fortunately most of new information created today is already in digital form and may just require conversion to formats appropriate to Digital library.

Digitisation projects have been important for libraries aiming the digitization of manuscripts, theses, dissertation, special collections which are special in nature. Every Libraries should Digitize their collection to provide a wide and dynamic access of their resources available to the users in effective way. It will provide solution to their several problems like space, preservation of old age and fragile materials, user's satisfaction, time etc. But the digitization initiatives in India are encountered with the problems of lack of technical infrastructure, trained manpower, finances and policy initiatives.

REFRENCES

- Bansode,Sadanand and Pujar,S.M, 2008. "Scholarly Digital Library Initiative:world Versus India" ,*DESIDOC Journal of Library and Information Technology.* Vol.28,no.6.pp.11-20. *www.publications.drdo.gov.in/ojs/index.php/djlit/article/download/219/122 (Accessed on 22 June 2014).*
- Gurram, Sujatha, 2008. "Digital library initiatives in India: a proposal for open distance learning".*Proceedings of the IATUL Conferences.* pp.1-13.www. docs.lib.purdue.edu/cgi/viewcontent.cgi?article=1859&context=iatul(Accessed on 6 July 2014).
- Li, Xiuqi and Furht, Borko. DESIGN AND IMPLEMENTATION OF DIGITAL LIBRARIES". *www.cse.fau.edu/~borko/Chapter18_ic.pdf* (Accessed on 24 June 2014).
- Lihitkar, Shalini R. and Ghade, Vibha A. "Study of Selected Digital Libraries at National level". www.eprints.rclis.org/14169/1/IMT,Digital_Library.pdf (Accessed on 24 June 2014).
- Mandal, Achintya K . and NANDI, SUBODH GOPAL, 2007. "Role of open source software to measure usage of digital library and its improvement : a case study". 5th International CALIBER. pp.776-787. *http://ir.inflibnet.ac.in/bitstream/1944/1452/1/776-787.pdf* (Accessed on 2 July 2014).
- S. N. Singh, Ngurtinkhuma,R K. and Pankaj Kumar Singh, 2007 "Open source software: a comparative study of greenstone and dspace",5th International CALIBER. pp.89-97. *http://ir.inflibnet.ac.in/bitstream/1944/517/1/89-97.pdf* (Accessed on 6 July 2014).
- *Sree Kumar, M.G and Sreejaya, P, 2005. "Digital Library Initiatives and Issues in India: efforts on scholarly knowledge management". www.dspace.iimk.ac.in/bitstream/2259/252/1/05-mgs-ps-paper.pdf* (Accessed on 24 June 2014).
- **Varatharajan, N. and Chandrashekara, M., 2007. "Digital Library Initiatives at Higher Education and Research**

Institutions in India", *Library Philosophy and Practice*. pp.1-7. *www.webpages.uidaho.edu/~mbolin/vara-chandra.pdf* (Accessed on 2 July 2014).

- www.shodhganga.inflibnet.ac.in/bitstream/10603/10294/.../10_chapter%201.p...; (Accessed on 4 July 2014).
- Tramboo, Shahkar et al. (2012)."A Study on the Open Source Digital Library Software's: Special Reference to DSpace, EPrints and Greenstone", International Journal of Computer Applications (0975 – 8887) . vol.59,no.16 .pp.1-9. www.*arxiv.org/pdf/1212.4935* (Accessed on 2 July 2014).

13

Library Classification in the 21st Century

Jivesh Bansal
Deputy Librarian, Panjab University Library,
Chandigarh-160014

ABSTRACT

Classification aims at creating an order out of chaos. It is the innate need of human beings to organize materials. Classification is the foundation of librarianship. Libraries organize their collections on the shelves with the help of classification. Classification schemes like DDC, LC and UDC were evolved for arrangement of physical materials like books on shelves. With the advancement of ICT, information resources are available in multiple formats. Millions of documents reside on internet. Classification is a tool of knowledge organisation systems. The networked media has brought many innovative methods of communication of information and posed many challenges to classification. The emergence of DDC, LC and UDC classification schemes in electronic form and then online availability is the most important development in library classification. Folksonomies, taxonomies, ontologies, tagging and social bookmarking have emerged as recent classification tools for internet documents. These recent classification developments have worked successfully towards knowledge organisation.

Keywords : Library Classification, Folksonomies, Web 2.0, Automatic Classification

1. INTRODUCTION

Human beings have the innate ability to classify things. Classification is simply grouping together of like entities based on some common characteristic. Library classification is the systematic arrangement of books on shelves. It aims at efficient retrieval of documents in quickest possible time. It is the foundation of librarianship and an important tool for knowledge organization. Library classification schemes are systematic and logical arrangement of subjects in schedules with notation representing these subjects. Library classification schemes are also being used to categorise electronic resources. Enumerative and Faceted are two species of Library Classification.

2. GENERAL CLASSIFICATION SCHEMES

(i) Dewey Decimal Classification : It was given by Melvil Dewey in 1876. It organizes the whole field of knowledge into ten main classes. DDC is available in both print and electronic versions and it has undergone continuous revisions and updations. DDC's coverage is comprehensive. DDC became available in electronic form in 1993. The Web Dewey was made available by OCLC in 2003.

(ii) Library of Congress Classification Scheme : It is developed and published by the Library of Congress, Washington, DC. The scheme has 47 separate schedules. Its publication can be traced back to 1897. It is enumerative scheme of classification. It is broadly divided into 21 categories labels spreading into A to Z, but the letters L,O,W,X,Y are unused.

(iii) Universal Decimal Classification : It was developed by Henri La Fontaine and Paul Otlet in 1905 from DDC. The whole universe of knowledge is organized into ten broad classes. It is highly flexible and effective system for organizing bibliographic records , books etc. UDC is suitable for specialist collection. UDC is available in many languages and is controlled by the Universal Decimal Classification Consortium (UDCC).

(iv) Colon Classification : It is a faceted scheme of classification developed by Dr. S.R.Ranganathan in 1933. It uses mixed notation. It is also called analytic-synthetic scheme of classification. Citation order is controlled by the facet formula PMEST.

Kumbhar (2012) has listed specific uses of classification:

- Use in arranging periodicals and browsing online catalogues.
- Use in organization of bibliographic entries.
- Use in collection development
- Use in reference service
- Use in information retrieval
- Use in thesaurus and taxonomy development
- Use in organizing web based information sources
- Use in classification of web pages
- Use in classification of search queries
- Use in classification of e-mails
- Use in knowledge representation
- Use in e-learning

3. RECENT TRENDS IN CLASSIFICATION

Advancement in information and communication technology has revolutionized the library profession. The technological developments and innovations resulted in the rapid production of documents, various tools for searching the documents, electronic publishing, etc. Millions of documents are sprawling on the internet. Heterogeneous sources of information reside on the internet.

Classification is a foundation of knowledge organization. It aims at resource organization and their efficient retrieval. But networked media i.e. resource organization on internet is a big challenge posed to classification. Traditional classification schemes require formal categories that do not change over time, controlled vocabularies, expert cataloguers, authoritative source, expert users. But heterogeneous sources of information on the internet are without a central authority. In these situations traditional classification schemes become ineffective. New trends that are emerging in classification are -

- General classification schemes in electronic form and web environment
- Automatic Classification
- Newer knowledge organization tools such as taxonomies, folksonomies, ontologies, etc.

Classification Schemes in Electronic Form or Web based Library Classification Schemes

In the emerging electronic environment in the 21st century, the library classification schemes evolved from print into the web version too. This dynamism marked a new chapter in library classification schemes. The web based library classification schemes are constantly updated and revised. These have many additional features (like easy access of schedules, use of hyperlinks, online retrieval of class numbers, time saving, etc.) which make them gain an edge over printed versions. The current web based library classification schemes are -

Web Dewey 2.0 (DDC23rd)

Web Dewey is a browser based version of the Dewey Decimal Classification database. Web Dewey 2.0 provides all the contents i.e. schedules, tables, manual, notes and relative index of DDC 23 or Abridged Web Dewey (Abridged DDC15). The salient features are -

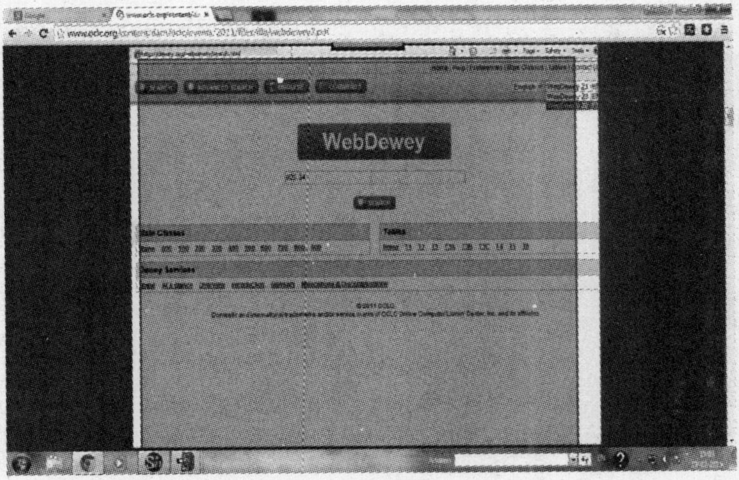

- Users can add their own notes, save and search their notes about local classification practices.
- Includes 'Relative Index' terms and built numbers not available in 'Printed DDC'
- Provides links to OPAC
- Provides additional search features and hyperlinks
- LCSH to DDC mappings
- Simple and easy to use

UDC Online

It is the web based version of the universal decimal classification. It is available on the web since 2001. The official text of the UDC is the Master Reference File, the database created and maintained by UDCC. The online edition of UDC is derived from Master Reference File. It is an enhanced version of the printed schedule.

- Provides search and browse facility.
- Number building facility to help construct complex UDC numbers.
- Ability for multiple search strategies

- Special auxiliaries are not shown separately. It is displayed with specific colour when search results are displayed.

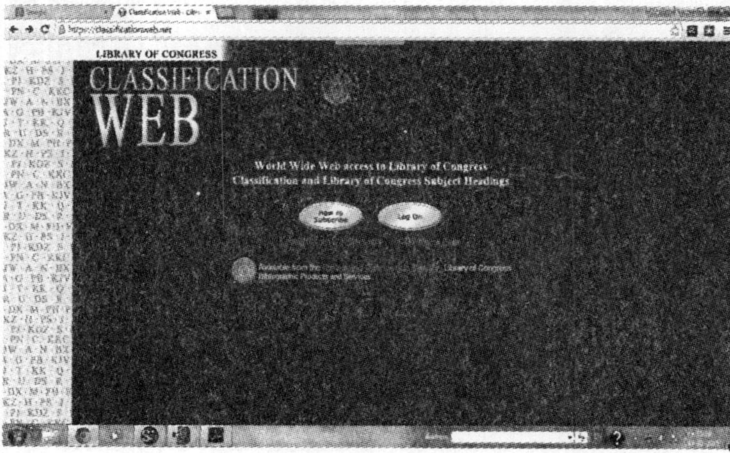

Library of Congress Classification Scheme or Classification Web LC Web

Classification web is a web based version of Library of Congress Classification Scheme. It helps the users to browse and search the full text of the Library of Congress Classification schedules. Classification web contains LCC schedules, LC class and its subdivisions, Library of Congress Subject Headings. Users can access the correlations between LCC numbers and LCSH and DDC

Users can create their own notes in the database. The scheme has ability to link to local Web OPAC for many major vendor systems.

4. AUTOMATIC CLASSIFICATION

Classification of documents is one of the prime function of libraries. The documents to be classified may be text, images, music etc. Automatic classification is doing classification with the help of computers. Automatic text classification is automatically categorising digital documents into pre-defined classes. According to Wijewickrema and Gamage (2013) Possible stages of automatic classification are -

First Stage

Stemming and removing stop words : It reduces the text to more useful text and removes less significant words from the input document. Using this output; the first few highly frequent terms are selected as key terms to determine the discipline of the document in focus (input document).

Training set : is a collection of documents where the training documents are stored. One can use them to compare with the input document to determine the subject of it. This can be done by evaluating the similarities between previously selected key terms of the input document and the terms in the training document.

Text Classification Algorithm : It is to numerically determine to what extent a given document relates to a particular subject.

Second Stage

Ontology : Domain ontology is used to reduce vocabulary ambiguities. Ontology can be constructed using DDC and Sears list.

Third Stage

- Filter all possible class classification results that are given by the system after the second stage so that user gets only one suggesting class number.

5. FOLKSONOMIES

The term 'Folksonomy' was coined by Thomas Vander Wal. It is composed of two words: Folks and Taxonomy. Therefore, it means people's classification management. It is a part of web 2.0. Users add tags/ labels of their choice to internet items i.e. images, websites etc. and use these tags for their own information retrieval purposes. It serves as a tool for their personal online information management. It is also termed as social classification, social tagging. It has social benefits. Other users can use these tags for previously undiscovered items. The characteristics of folkosomomies are -

- No hierarchy in tags.
- Intended to make a body of information increasingly easier to search, discover, and navigate over time.
- A well developed folksonomy is accessible as a shared vocabulary that is both originated by, and familiar to its primary users"- Wikipedia
- Serendipity- It is possible to discover all items which were having same tag, even used by other users.
- Tag cloud- Tag clouds are shown on popular tags showing their frequency of use.

Folksonomies consist of three basic entities- users, tags and resource. Users create tags to mark resources such as web pages, images, videos, etc. These tags are used to manage, categorize and summarize online content. Folksonomy is of two types - Broad and Narrow. *Broad folksonomy* is one in which multiple users tag particular content with a variety of terms from a variety of vocabularies, thus creating a greater amount of metadata for that content. *Narrow folksonomy* is one in which few user primarily the content creator , tag an object with a limited number of terms. Examples of Folksonomies are – Photograph Sharing Website Flickr, Social Bookmarking Website Del.icio.us, etc.

Flickr : (http;//www.flickr.com) is a social photo managementand sharing tool that allows users to easily upload and share digital photos. It requires users to create a user account and is free to join. Flickr has a number of options to upload photographs to the system through WebPagesand software applications. Tags can be added at the time of upload, or later in the process when the photographs are displayed by the system.

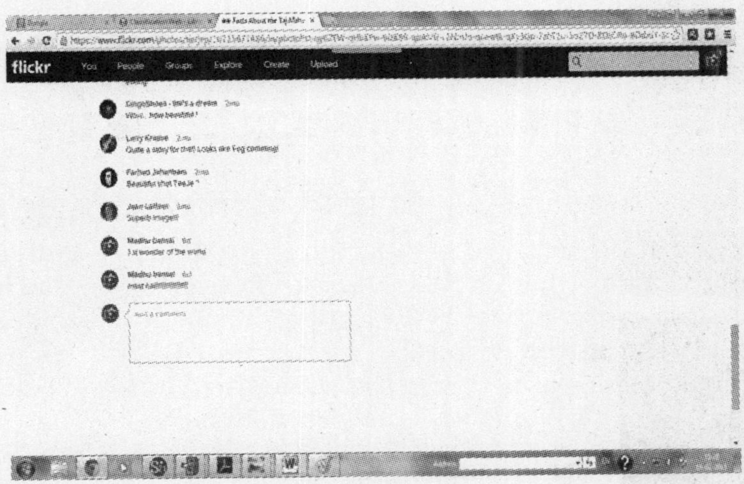

Del.icio.us

It is a social bookmark manager. It allows user to add webpages to personal collections, to tag them, and to share their collections with others. User can access bookmarks on any computer-no need to remember whether user bookmarked a website at home or office computer. User can also look at the websites others have tagged, and the most popular and recent tags. These websites are also called social bookmarking websites.

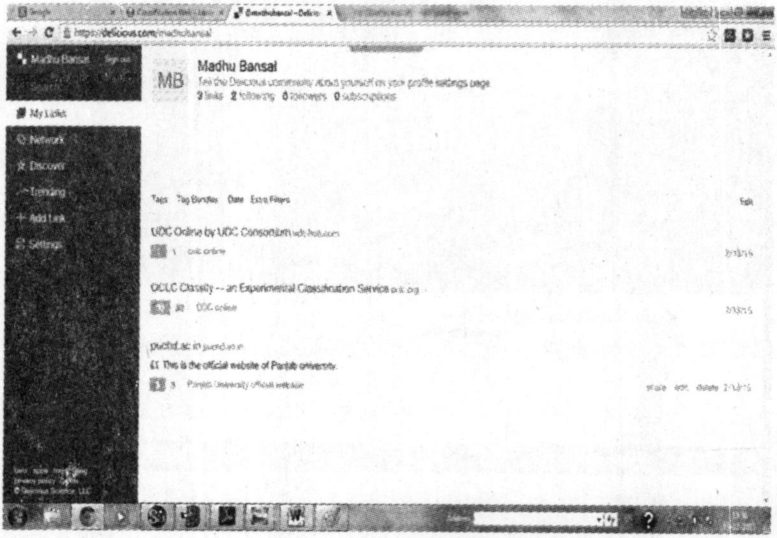

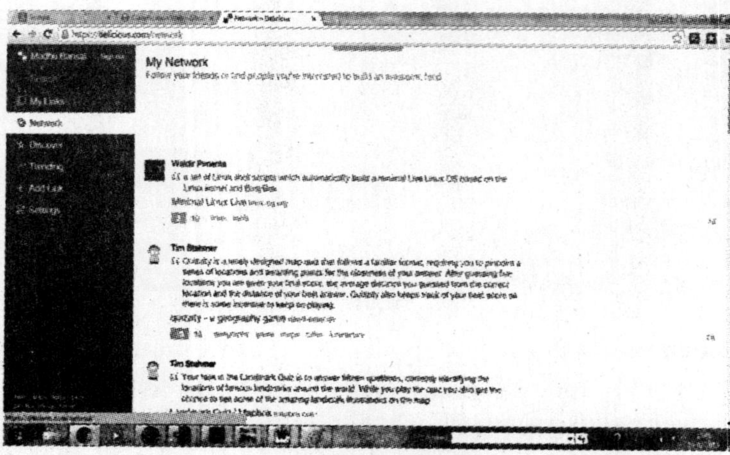

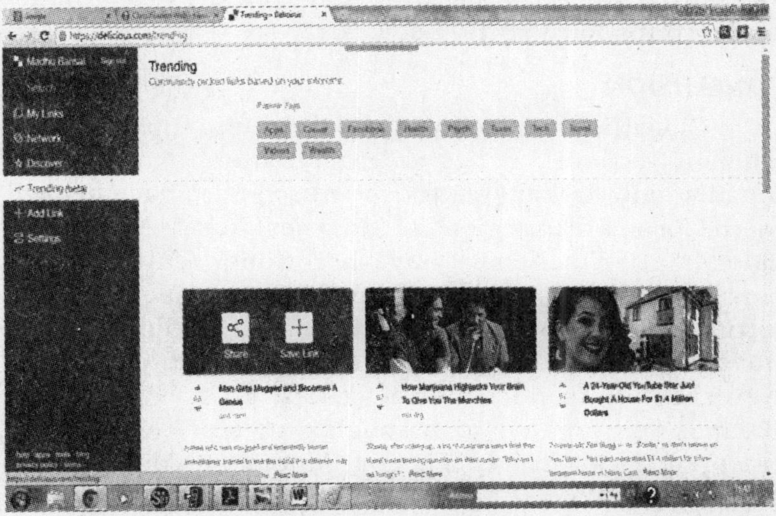

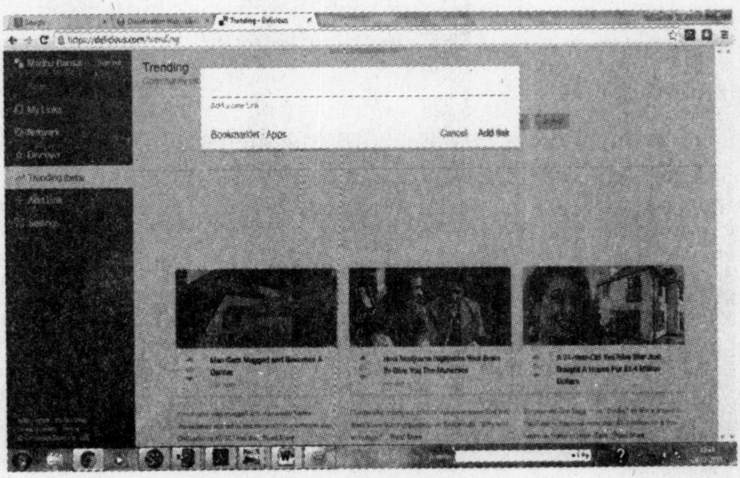

Folkonomy has many benefits such as -

- Communities are formed within content subject.
- Users can find who tagged content and follow other tags by that person.

- Interesting groups form and members of various groups form social networks.

CONCLUSION

Classification aims at resource organization for efficient retrieval. It lies at grass-roots of knowledge-organisation. Library classification schemes have helped in the best arrangement of libraries. Web versions of classification schemes have additional features like constant updation, easy access of schedules, online retrieval of class-numbers, and use of hyperlinks which have an added advantage over printed versions. Heterogeneous documents reside on the internet. Harmony is created in managing these resources by emerging trends in classification. Automatic classification and use of Web 2.0 tools are the recent trends in classification that have justifiably managed the internet resources. These aim to organize the chaos of information and retrieve relevant information later on.

REFERENCES

Batley, S., 2005. *Classification in theory and practice.* Oxford: Chandos Pub.

Crawford, L., 2011. Wed Dewey 2.0. *www.oclc.org/content/dam/oclc/events/2011/files/ifla/webdewey2.pdf* (Accessed on January 10, 2015)

Knoll, G. (n.d.). Folksonomy: Tagging. *http://www.cs.colorado.edu/~kena/classes/7818/f06/lectures/folksonomy.pdf* (Accessed on January 18, 2015)

Kumbhar, R., 2012. *Library classification trends in the 21stcentury.* New Delhi: Chandos Pub., 10-24.

Library of Congress (n.d.). Classification Web. *http://www.classificationweb.net/* (Accessed on January 15, 2015)

OCLC (n.d.). Web Dewey. *http://dewey.org/webdewey* (Accessed on January 12, 2015)

Quintarrelli, E. (2005). Folksonomies: power to the people. *http://www.iskoi.org/doc/folksonomies.htm* (Accessed on January 18, 2015)

UDC Consortium (n.d.). UDC Online. *http://www.udc-hub.com/* (Accessed on January 10, 2015)

Wijewickrema, C. M., & Gamage, R. (2013). An ontology based fully automatic document classification system using an existing semi-automatic system. *http://library.ifla.org/159/1/112-wijewickrema-en.pdf* (Accessed on January 15, 2015)